THE COMPLETE BOOK OF

FORMS

FOR MANAGING THE SCHOOL LIBRARY MEDIA CENTER

Ruth Toor, M.L.S. and
Hilda K. Weisburg, M.L.S.

The Center for Applied Research in Education, Inc.
West Nyack, New York 10994

Library of Congress Cataloging in Publication Data

Toor, Ruth, 1933–
      The complete book of forms for managing the school library media center.

      Includes index.
          1. School libraries—Forms.
      2. Instructional materials centers—Forms.
      I. Weisburg, Hilda K., 1942–
      II. Title.
      Z675.S3T585 1982   027.8   82-9674
      ISBN 0-87628-229-X

Printed in the United States of America

To our fathers—
They would have been proud
John Arak 1903–1971
Lawrence Kaplan 1910–1979

About the Authors

Ruth Toor, M.L.S. and Hilda K. Weisburg, M.L.S. are coauthors of the *Elementary School Librarian's Almanac* (West Nyack, N.Y.: The Center for Applied Research in Education, Inc., 1979) and coeditors of the *School Librarian's Workshop*, a practical monthly professional aid for practicing library media specialists. They have been featured panelists and speakers at state, county and local conferences and workshops for library media specialists and teachers.

Ruth Toor earned her B.A. from the University of Delaware and her M.L.S. from Rutgers University, and is continuing further graduate education in computer sciences and media. Currently a library media specialist at Southern Boulevard School in Chatham Township, New Jersey, she has also done consulting on media center programs and facilities and served as head of the State Intellectual Freedom Committee and is vice president of the State Educational Media Association. She and her husband have two grown sons.

Hilda K. Weisburg earned her M.L.S. from Columbia University as a specialist in Children's and Young Adult Services. She is continuing graduate studies in computer sciences and management. At present she is the library media specialist at both the Harry S. Truman School and Dwight D. Eisenhower School in Sayreville, New Jersey, and served on the State Task Force on Standards. She lives with her husband and their two energetic teenagers.

About this Book
of Library Management Aids

The Complete Book of Forms for Managing the School Library Media Center gives you, the library media specialist, a one-stop source for all of the forms needed to manage today's media center. Included are over 170 ready-to-use forms—most of which can be reproduced from the pages of this book—to help you in virtually every aspect of your work, from assessing physical facilities and materials, organizing staff and programs, and communicating with administrators and the community, to analyzing your own professional needs and development. You will find a wealth of material covering the traditional forms in their many guises as well as new ways to document the wide variety of programs and services performed at this time when accountability requirements pose so many problems.

The varied formats used for the forms offer alternative ways to approach your particular management problems in any school—elementary or secondary. You can use or adapt these aids to suit your own situation. In this way, your media center will be given the advantage of acquiring an individually tailored form without your having to spend valuable time designing it. Where it is necessary to demonstrate the use of a form, a filled-in sample is provided in the introduction of the particular section. A blank, ready-to-use form for most of these samples is then provided at the end of that section. A directory of commerical sources of library forms can be found in the Appendix.

This book is organized to allow you to control your surroundings, maintain and manage services, handle administrative details, and record all of your activities. The book's sections follow the sequence of the school year, from Sections 1 and 2, which help you document beginning-of-the-year activities, through Section 9, which helps you organize the close of the media center at the end of the year. Here's a general description of all ten sections:

Sections 1 and 2:   Organizational preliminaries to start the year

Sections 3 and 4:   Practices that support the programs and services

Sections 5 and 6:   Documenting programs and services to students and teachers

Sections 7 and 8:   Professional responsibilities within and without the school district

Section 9:   Organizing the end of the year, the complement to Sections 1 and 2

Section 10:   Personal professional growth and development

Some of the unique and particularly useful features of this book of library management aids are:

- Money-saving alternatives to commercially produced forms
- Forms designed for easy duplication by machine
- A quick and easy analysis of media center holdings
- Ways to organize and schedule support staff whether it be paid, volunteer, or student
- Forms to control and monitor media circulation
- Ways to document work with teachers
- Forms and letters for handling complaints
- Checklists of what you need to know from your administration
- New ideas for programs and how to record them
- How to get your message out to parents and the community effectively
- You and the job market
- Unique forms unavailable elsewhere

With this collection of forms in hand, you will find that you can easily control a large volume of clerical and professional recordkeeping. Consult the section needed and choose the form best suited to your purpose. You, the time-conscious professional, will be able to use this book as a ready reference to stay on top of the many demands made on today's media center.

Ruth Toor
Hilda K. Weisburg

Contents

3. Forms for Circulation Control **61**

The media center generates an enormous amount of paper work. The forms in this section will help you control the clerical interaction between the media center and its users, allowing student access, dealing with circulation problems such as overdues, reserves, lost books and charge-out procedures, and recording the statistics of these operations.

4. Forms for Technical Services 111

Technical services include the selection, acquisition, and maintenance of the collection. This behind-the-scenes activity requires careful management to allow the media center to function smoothly. Under optimal conditions, your patrons are generally unaware of the existence of this operation, although it is one of the most critical areas of professional responsibility.

5. Forms for Managing Library Programs 123

A media center is ultimately judged by its programs. Everything else exists to allow these services to run effectively. This section focuses on working directly with students in the media center. While teachers are encouraged to participate, the emphasis here is on your interaction with individual students, small groups, and entire classes, which culminates in a school-wide book fair. The forms provided will help you accurately record services and programs that are normally hard to document for administrative purposes.

6. Forms for Working with Teachers

You must constantly interrelate with your teachers to effectively develop programs and to enhance students' skills. The forms in this section will help you record the two-way communication that must exist. They include schedules, notification of happenings, classroom aids, and teacher feedback.

7. Forms for Working with the Administration

The administration controls the environment in which you work. It establishes the limits of your decision-making, the methods you may use for making selections and purchases, and the funds you have available. To operate efficiently you must know and have a record of these boundaries and how to comply with them. The forms in this section include your record of district policies and samples of your reports and requests to the administration.

8. Forms for Correspondence 189

You must frequently communicate with the world outside your school system. Explanations, complaints, requests, and thank-you notes require your attention. This section provides samples of how to get the word out succinctly.

9. Forms for End-of-Year Activities 207

Closing the media center for summer vacation requires tight organization, close scheduling, and extra help. The forms in this section for scheduling, recalling, and inventorying materials and equipment will allow you to retain control. Forms are also provided for a culminating activity—a thank-you party or trip that will give your helpers an incentive for future service.

You have a responsibility to maintain the standards of your profession. To fulfill this obligation, you must stay current with changes in librarianship and promote your own abilities forthrightly. The forms in this section include a resume and job application plus personal records of courses taken, conventions attended, and demonstrations of professional expertise.

Section 1

Forms for Analyzing Your Facilities and Collection

I THINK THIS MAP IS FOR ANOTHER SCHOOL.

As you begin the school year, take stock of your surroundings and gain control of the situation. Managing a modern media center requires that you have a multitude of information at your fingertips. Whether you are a new media specialist or an experienced practitioner, at a new school or at one you've served for several years, get organized by collecting the basic data you need.

Forms give you a sense of order and structure. They provide a point of reference that permits comparison and indicates direction. Without forms you will have difficulty remembering what you have done, justifying your function, and evaluating the degree of your success.

As you collect information, begin recording it on the forms shown here. Eliminate, modify, and create new forms as your situation dictates and your management experience broadens. These forms give you an overview of the resources you can use to analyze the physical plant, your collection (both book and nonbook), audio-visual equipment, and all supplies.

MEDIA CENTER FLOOR PLAN (FORM 1-1)

Try to get the architect's floor plan of the media center. It will be the most accurate as to scale. Be prepared to correct it as you do your inspection. The sample floor plan shown in Form 1-1 is not an illustration of the final arrangements. The screen was later moved to the reference section. No low tables were placed in the magazine area, and other minor modifications were made.

If you cannot get the architect's drawing, make your own. Use the grid in Form 1-1 at the end of this section to help you keep the proportions correct. Later, transfer the drawing to unlined paper for easier reading. Include all shelving, furniture, location of doors, windows, stairs, and all other physical features. With the floor plan in hand, tour the media center to fix the details

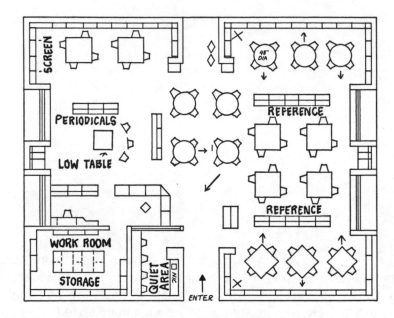

FORM 1-1   Sample Media Center Floor Plan

in your mind. Notice areas that are difficult to supervise. Check for poor seating arrangements and fire exits. In Form 1-1, x's have been placed to indicate areas that are difficult to see from the desk. Arrows have been placed by the tables that need to be moved. In the arrangement shown here, students might move their chairs back, causing frequent collisions and upsetting the atmosphere.

Walk through the steps of returning books, making selections, and charging out materials to see if traffic flows naturally. Discipline problems often arise because of a poor layout. Anticipation and prevention might eliminate difficulties before they surface.

PHYSICAL FACILITIES CHECKLIST (FORM 1-2)

While you tour the media center with the floor plan, take along your Physical Facilities Checklist, Form 1-2. Since furniture may occasionally be borrowed by teachers and custodians during the course of the year, you need to know what belongs to you. You also need to be aware of the number of students you can accommodate at any one time. This information will aid your later planning for large and small groups. Decide how big a group you can work with before you must close the media center to other students.

Library cooperation programs need communication. A telephone is the first link. Vertical files need furniture or creative librarianship. Do you have the files or the space for them? What type of display area do you have—cases, bulletin boards, countertops?

SCHOOL FLOOR PLAN (FORM 1-3)

See how the media center fits into the school building plan, a sample of which is shown in Form 1-3. Which grade levels or subject areas are closest and which are farthest away? You will need to make a point of establishing communication with those geographically distant from you.

Where are the storage areas located? How convenient are they for rapidly setting up audio-visual stations to supply different sections of the building? Don't neglect fire alarm boxes on your diagram. You and your staff must be familiar with this basic device. Accidents do occur; you must be prepared.

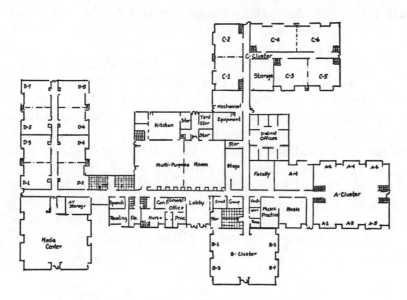

FORM 1-3   Sample School Floor Plan

FORMS FOR ANALYZING THE COLLECTION

Quick Survey of Book Collection (Form 1-4)

Use Form 1-4 to get an immediate overview of your collection. You rarely have the time to make an exact count, but you should have an idea of the size and scope of your resources. By simply counting the number of shelves per classification and multiplying the figure by the average number of books per shelf, you will obtain a reasonable estimate of each area.

Form 1-4 allows you to include any special collections. Separate areas for holiday books, autographed books, state material, occupational centers, and so on could be recorded here. Note under "comments" any great strengths or serious weaknesses that must be remedied.

Categorical Survey of Periodicals and Newspapers (Forms 1-5—1-7)

Taking a count of periodical holdings is easy, but it provides little useful information. It is far more informative to make an analysis by category using Form 1-5. Make preliminary judgments now, subject to change as the year progresses, and you will see how the magazines are used. For example, you might originally put *National Geographic* in the general-interest category along with *Seventeen* and *Boy's Life*. However, if the science department requires reports from this magazine, change the category to "Science." By analyzing your holdings this way, you can judge strengths and weaknesses readily.

Maintain a complete alphabetical listing of periodical/newspaper holdings with Form 1-6. Use this record to keep track of expiration dates, whether a publication is ordered directly or from a jobber, and whether you intend to reorder it or not. This will help you with next year's order by pulling all of the pertinent information together in one place.

To increase the cost-effectiveness of periodical purchasing, it is advisable to establish a Simple Union List of Serials, Form 1-7. Include the holdings of every school in the district to facilitate interlibrary loans. Use code letters to indicate which school holds which subscriptions. The category designation correlates with that used on Form 1-5. It is most helpful to know how long back copies are kept and whether they are available on microform. The union list can be a preliminary to a larger library cooperation project.

SURVEYS OF HARDWARE AND SOFTWARE

In discussing audio-visual material, it is simplest to begin by defining the terms "hardware" and "software":

- *Hardware* refers to equipment. It is unchangeable. Record players, cassette players, projectors, television monitors, and so on are all forms of hardware.
- *Software* refers to the programs used on the hardware. A variety of software programs can be used with any given piece of hardware. Records

are software, as are filmstrips, transparencies, and video cassettes. The program sent out on the hardware is changed by changing the software.

Hardware Inventories (Forms 1-8, 1-9)

To maintain hardware, you need a supply of lamps and batteries and other small items. Do not confuse these materials with software. They are a part of hardware maintenance. The terms "lamps" and "bulbs" are not synonymous. All bulbs are lamps, but the reverse is not true. Bulbs refer specifically to those lamps having a bulbous shape. Tubular lights can be described only as lamps.

To maintain service without a disproportionate amount of downtime (time lost while equipment is being repaired), it is necessary to keep a basic inventory of lamps, batteries, and needles. Use Form 1-8 to list what you have on hand. Batteries include those needed for cameras and camera flash attachments. Although needles are not mentioned specifically, do enter them here.

When you are new to a building, you may have difficulty anticipating the "Number to Order," the heading of the last column of Form 1-8. As a general rule, you need fewer lamps per projector as the number of projectors increases. To become reasonably accurate in predicting needs, you must learn your school's individual rate of use. The form has a place for the date the inventory is taken. This will serve as a record of the year's consumption. You can predict future orders by using this as a guide. After a few years, your estimates will become very accurate.

Since hardware is the first item to circulate from the media center, it is imperative to have accurate records of holdings even before the school year begins. No matter how difficult, complete Form 1-9 before doing anything else. Once the equipment is scattered around the building, you will have to spend hours tracking it down and your list will invariably still miss something.

When you use Form 1-9, enter the type of equipment first (for example, "16mm projector"), then list all brands owned, such as Bell & Howell, Eiki, and so on. If you have a lot of hardware, you may decide to use one Form 1-9 per type of equipment. In that case, enter the name of the appropriate equipment next to "Hardware Inventory" to make your filing easier.

The narrow column next to the heading "Model Number" is given so you can make a check mark if you own a user's manual. When lamp or battery changes or cleaning become necessary, it is helpful to know whether you have a copy of accurate directions or whether you need to make intelligent guesses. The list of serial numbers is obviously required in case of loss or damage. The code number is the number you assign to the hardware to simplify circulation, which is similar to a book's accession number. Use the last column to cross-check with Form 1-8. This will ensure that you own all items necessary to support the basic functioning of the equipment.

Survey of Software (Form 1-10)

Your media center collection refers to software as well as to books. To determine the scope of your resources, you need to analyze these holdings in the same way that you analyzed your book collection.

Form 1-10 allows you to make a qualitative as well as a quantitative assessment. You may give the job of entering the numbers to any staff member. Use the shelf list if you are sure that it is accurate, or, if circulation has not yet begun, go directly to the shelves. The column labeled "Other" is used for those materials either uncataloged or not assigned a Dewey number. One caution: Do not be alarmed by a preponderance of 300s. Commercial software catalogers are notorious for classifying almost everything in the 370s under "Education." The comments section permits you to make a few notations about the strengths, weaknesses, and perceived needs.

SUPPLY CHECKLISTS (FORMS 1-11—1-15)

Service is your function, but nothing moves without supplies. Although your administration may seem totally unaware of the variety of office and stationery items as well as the specifically library-oriented supplies that are vital to the media center, you cannot overlook them. The four checklists provide you with an overall survey of what's on hand and what you need immediately. Each checklist is dated to help you anticipate future orders. When you have good records, budget requests are simplified. These checklists also serve an extra benefit as a documentation of the wide range of tasks you oversee and carry out.

Form 1-11 is a record of supplies needed for processing and circulation. Under each form heading, list the items noted below.

Catalog cards: number on hand and type, for example, color-banded, unlined, red-lined

Book cards: amount on hand and color as well as special types, such as periodical book cards

Book pockets: number and type that may have high or low backs

Date due notices: cards or miniature slips, depending on what your media center uses

Periodical record cards: daily and monthly records

Rubber stamps: space is provided for number of property, reference, date, accession, and federal title fund stamps, plus whatever special ones you might use

Stamp pads: indicate color and note if you have replacement inkers for the pads

Labels: list amounts, sizes, and types, including subject labels such as "mysteries," "sports," and "science fiction" to go on book spines; do not include a-v labels here—they go on Form 1-12

Notices: overdue notices, reserve notices, and library passes

Circulation records: daily and annual circulation records

Other: Your own media center needs are paramount here. The list includes book jackets, order cards, I.L.L. forms, signal flags for book/catalog cards, transfer tape, plastic spray, and date cards for the circulation file.

Form 1-12 records maintenance and storage supplies.

Tapes come in a wide variety of types, widths, and materials. Clear tape alone comes in cellophane and mylar as well as a variety of widths. For hinge tape, there are different types of perforations as well as single and double hinges.

Paste comes as library white and adhesive. There is also rubber cement.

Under "Book Ends," list only those not in current use. The idea here is to know what you have available. If they are now holding up books, they are not readily available.

Files include princeton and cut files.

Media storage boxes are, once again, those on hand, not those in use. List the types, such as cassette, filmstrip/cassette, transparency, and so on.

Binders for pamphlets and periodicals should go under "Other," as should plastic jackets for record albums, package sealing tape, mending kits, and bone folders.

Form 1-13 looks like any office supply checklist. In running a media center you are also operating an office. Although the need for them may not be as obvious at first, these very basic supplies are just as important as all the others. Be sure to check what you have on hand.

When compiling this list, be sure you have an ample supply of file folders because you will need them for your vertical file as well. Under "Other" include typewriter cleaner, lined paper, pads, address labels, chalk, erasers, and so on.

Form 1-14 is an unusual supply list because it not only tells you what supplies you have on hand and what you need to order, but it also indicates services falling under your responsibility. Remember that when these in-house productions have been completed, they must then be cataloged and placed into regular circulation. Taking an annual survey will give you a clear perspective of your school's needs. The "Other" column under "Transparencies" gives you room to list transparency pencils, sprays, mounts, and so on.

Date _____	HARRY S. TRUMAN SCHOOL Supply Requisition Form									
Chalk										
Staples										
Pencils										
Erasers										
Paper—Primary										
—Yellow										
—Composition										
Rubber Bands										
Rulers										

FORM 1-15   Sample Supply Requisition Form

Office supplies recorded in Form 1-13 are sometimes obtainable from general school supplies. Particularly if you are new to a building, it is wise to determine which supplies you may requisition from general storage and which must be included in your own budget. If any supplies are available within the school, a form is frequently needed. Form 1-15 is a typical example of the very simple ones in use. Check to see if your school requires one, and if so, keep a supply on hand.

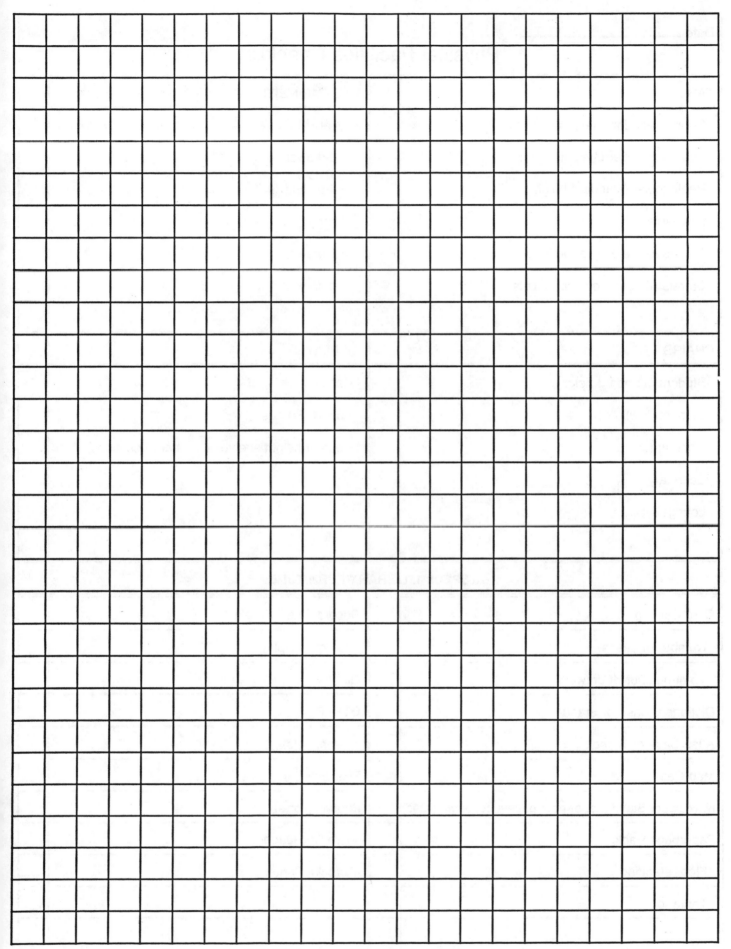

☐ =1 foot

Date _____

Physical Facilities Checklist

TABLES		FILE CABINETS	
Round (standard height)		Legal	
Square (standard height)		2-drawer	
Rectangular (standard height)		4-drawer	
Low tables		Letter	
Carrels with electrical outlets		2-drawer	
Carrels without electrical outlets		4-drawer	
CHAIRS		DISPLAY	
Student (standard height)		Cases	
Student (low)		Bulletin Boards	
Librarian(s)		Counter height shelves (number of sections)	
Secretary			
Lounge type			

SPECIAL LIBRARY FURNITURE

Card Catalog		Record Bins—Display	
Number of cases		Cassette Display	
Total number of drawers		Globes	
Dictionary Case or Stand		OTHER	
Atlas Case or Stand		Telephone(s)	
Map Case		Typewriter(s)	
Newspaper Stand (no. of newspapers accommodated)		Photocopier(s)	
Paperback Racks		Microfilm Reader	
Floor standing		Microfilm Printer	
Table top			

FORM 1-2   Physical Facilities Checklist

Date _____

Quick Survey of Book Collection

NONFICTION	Number of Shelves	Average Number Books per Shelf	Approximate Total
000's			
100's			
200's			
300's			
400's			
500's			
600's			
700's			
800's			
900's			
BIOGRAPHY			
Total			
REFERENCE			
Total			
FICTION			
Picture Books			
Total			
SPECIAL COLLECTION(S)			
PROFESSIONAL COLLECTION			
Grand Total			
COMMENTS: Strengths			
Weaknesses			

Date _____

Categorical Survey of Periodicals/Newspapers

PERIODICALS	TOTAL NUMBER	NUMBER INDEXED
General Interest		
Sports		
Science		
Current Events		
Art		
Literature		
Foreign Language		
Hobby/Recreation		
Other		
Total		
Professional		
Grand Total		

NEWSPAPERS		NUMBER RECEIVED
National		
Local		

Comments

Date _____   Page ____ of ____

List of Periodical/Newspaper Holdings

PERIODICAL/NEWSPAPER	EXPIRATION DATE	FREQUENCY of ISSUE	JOBBER or DIRECT	√IF INDEXED	REORDER? YES/NO

Date _____

Page ____ of ____

Simple Union List of Serials

PERIODICAL/NEWSPAPER	Schools Ordering	Category or Department Requesting	Number of Years Back Issue	On Micro-Form?

FORM 1-7   Simple Union List of Serials

Date _____

Hardware Maintenance Inventory

Lamp/Battery	Equipment—Type and Model	Number on Hand	Number to Order

Date _____

Hardware Inventory

Equipment Type	Brand	Model No.	✓	Serial Number	Code Number	Lamp or Battery

FORM 1-9   Hardware Inventory

Date _____

Survey of Software

Type	000	100	200	300	400	500	600	700	800	900	Other	Total
KITS												
FILMSTRIPS												
Sound												
Silent												
AUDIO MATERIALS												
Cassettes												
Sets												
Singles												
RECORDS												
Albums												
Singles												
VIDEO MATERIALS												
Tapes												
Cassettes												
16mm FILMS												
8mm LOOPS												
SLIDES												
Commercial												
In-House Produced												
TRANSPARENCIES												
Commercial												
In-House Produced												

Comments:

Date _____

Supply Checklist—Processing and Circulation

ITEM	On Hand	To Order	ITEM	On Hand	To Order
CATALOG CARDS			STAMP PADS		
			LABELS		
BOOK CARDS					
			NOTICES		
BOOK POCKETS					
			CIRCULATION RECORDS		
DATE DUE NOTICES					
			OTHER		
PERIODICAL RECORD CARDS					
RUBBER STAMPS					

Date _____

Supply Checklist—Maintenance and Storage

ITEM	On Hand	To Order	ITEM	On Hand	To Order
CLEAR TAPE			FILES		
CLOTH TAPE			MEDIA STORAGE BOXES		
			A-V LABELS		
HINGE TAPE					
			A-V CLEANING EQUIPMENT		
PASTE					
			OTHER		
BOOK WINGS					
BOOK ENDS					

Date _____

Supply Checklist—Office Supplies

ITEM	On Hand	To Order	ITEM	On Hand	To Order
STATIONERY			TAPE		
Letterhead Paper			STICK GLUE		
Letterhead Envelopes			RULERS		
Typing Paper			SCISSORS		
Blank Envelopes			STAPLER		
CARBON PAPER			STAPLES		
TYPEWRITER RIBBONS			RUBBER BANDS		
LIQUID PAPER			PUSH PINS		
DITTO MASTERS					
DITTO CORRECTION TAPE			PAPER CLIPS		
STENCILS					
STYLUS					
STENCIL CORRECTION FLUID			POSTAGE STAMPS		
PENCILS					
PENS					
			OTHER		
FELT MARKERS					
Fine-Line					
Broad-Tip					
ERASERS					
FILE FOLDERS					
Letter Size					
Legal Size					

FORM 1-13   Supply Checklist—Office Supplies

Date _____

Supply Checklist—In-House Media Production

TRANSPARENCIES

ACETATE	On Hand	Order	OTHER	On Hand	Order
PENS: washable					
permanent					

RECORDINGS
Audio/Video

BLANK AUDIO CASSETTES	On Hand	Order	HEAD CLEANERS	On Hand	Order
			AUDIO		
			VIDEO		
			DEMAGNETIZERS		
REEL-TO-REEL TAPE			SPLICERS		
BLANK VIDEO CASSETTES/TAPES					

FILM

TYPE	Amount on Hand	CAMERA	MAILERS	Order

DRY-MOUNT

MOUNTING TISSUE (sizes)	On Hand	Order	TACKING IRON	On Hand	Order
			SPRAY		

Section 2

Forms for Developing Personnel Relationships and Organizing Clerical/Volunteer Staff

I WONDER WHICH ONE IS MY BEST FOOT?

Now that you have gained control of the physical resources, it is time to focus your attention on the human resources. Your primary responsibility is to provide service. While you will eventually serve the entire school population, you offer help first to the instructional and support staffs. As the school year begins, these individuals are busy organizing their own areas. Step forward, meet the school personnel, and offer your help and service. Establish an immediate rapport with the staff, showing them how valuable your help can be to their programs. This effort sets the stage for an ongoing cooperative relationship which will blossom as the resources of the media center become integrated with the teaching program.

Accomplishing such an ambitious program requires a support staff in the media center. Help may be obtained in a variety of ways, but usually the organizational responsibility is yours. The forms in this chapter give you a sequential plan of action so that by the end of the first few weeks of school you will be fully operational and the year's activities will be successfully launched.

NEEDS SURVEYS (FORMS 2-1, 2-2)

Learn the names of the teachers quickly and get to meet them on an informal basis by using Form 2-1. Even if you know many of them already, take the opportunity to remind them of your presence. Become aware of their current marital status because when you send messages to them by way of students you should address the teachers correctly. By learning first names, if you don't already know them, you develop the easy camaraderie necessary for daily communication. Although learning names and room numbers is essential, don't lose sight of your main objective, which is to provide service. Find out what each teacher plans to use for an opening unit. You can then deliver the resources to help the teacher start the year impressively.

Staff members other than classroom teachers also need your services. To complete Form 2-2, meet all of the special teachers as well as the nurse, secretaries, and custodians. If any of them have aides, also record their names. Give the support personnel the chance to talk to you about their special problems and areas where media resources can be of help.

As you meet all the people in the school, fill in their names on the school floor plan, a sample of which is shown in Form 1-3. This will reinforce your mental image of where teachers are located and of their physical relationship to one another.

Job Description and Interviewing Forms (Forms 2-3—2-6)

Interviewing candidates for clerical positions and making hiring recommendations are rarely part of your responsibilities. However, administrators vary considerably in delegating tasks, and it is possible that you will be asked to aid in the selection of the media center staff.

Before any job announcement is made, you must be sure you know what position is being offered. A media clerk (formerly library clerk) is expected to have good typing skills and a familiarity with general clerical procedures. A media aide is one who has had training and/or experience in operating all the equipment and can produce slides, graphics, and transparencies to meet the needs of the media center's users. In a high school, students may be trained as media aides. A media technician is responsible for the maintenance and repair of a-v hardware and also can perform all the duties of a media aide. The technician may have an associate degree from a two-year college.

If you are to be deeply involved in the ultimate hiring decision, check with the administration to see if a job description is on file. Anyone interested in the position has the right to know exactly what will be required of him or her. The job description forms the basis for work evaluation; so if none exists, it is imperative that one be written. The board of education should vote on the description to make it legally binding. If time constraints make a board ruling impossible, get written approval or at least have the proposed job description you wrote initialed by the superintendent of schools.

Written job descriptions for media personnel are readily available. One excellent source is *Occupational Definitions for School Library Media Personnel* by the School Library Manpower Project (American Library Association, Chicago, 1971). The descriptions are detailed and run several pages, explaining the job, the nature and scope of the position, the major duties, and the required knowledge and abilities. You will undoubtedly wish to streamline and refine the descriptions to suit your own needs. Another source is state civil service job descriptions for public libraries, easily obtainable from your local library. This source needs only minor modifications to be used in school media centers.

Despite its importance, writing a job description is not difficult if you have a clear picture of what the position entails. For maximum flexibility, keep it brief and general.

Because the job of media clerk is often opened and filled quickly, you will probably have little time to prepare a job description for that position. See Form 2-3 for a sample you can easily adapt. Note that item 5 under "Requirements" may need to be changed for some districts. It may be ended after the word "volunteers" or a second language may be added. The term "school-acceptable English" means that any employee coming into contact with students should speak to them at a level judged acceptable in the class. Students need positive, not negative role models.

With the job description written, the position advertised, and applications submitted, interviewing can begin. According to most personnel management experts, the interview is a most ineffective predictor of job success. Nonetheless no one ever wants to hire a person sight unseen. To minimize the influence of looks and mannerisms on your decision, plan an interview schedule, using a written list of questions that are asked of all applicants. By following one, you will not let personal likes and dislikes cause you to neglect certain questions.

Remember, there are many questions you may not ask in the interview. It is a violation of federal law to ask the applicant's age, race, or religion. No questions may be asked about arrests, although you can ask about convictions.

JOB DESCRIPTION

TITLE: Media Clerk

GENERAL DESCRIPTION: The media clerk performs clerical tasks in the media center, including but not limited to typing and filing catalog cards, processing media materials, and performing basic maintenance of equipment all under the supervision of the library media specialist. The media clerk promotes the philosophy of the media center.

REQUIREMENTS:
1. Must comply with all employment criteria legally established by the board of education.
2. Must be able to type 50–60 words per minute.
3. Must be able to file alphabetically and numerically.
4. Must be willing to learn to operate and do basic maintenance of media center equipment.
5. Must be able to communicate with students, faculty, administrators and volunteers in school-acceptable English.
6. Must have a positive attitude toward media center programs.

MAJOR DUTIES:
1. Type all letters, reports, notices, and catalog cards prepared by the library media specialist.
2. File catalog cards.
3. Prepare books, periodicals, and media software for circulation.
4. Inspect new equipment to determine if it is functioning properly.
5. Change lamps and batteries in equipment.
6. Clean equipment periodically.
7. Maintain circulation file.
8. Assist in training volunteers under the direction of the library media specialist.
9. Assist students, faculty, and administration in locating materials in the media center.
10. May prepare displays and bulletin boards.
11. Comply with all requests of the library media specialist that fall within generally accepted clerical responsibilities.

FORM 2-3   Sample Job Description—Media Clerk

If the applicant has young children, you may not ask how he or she plans to cope if the children are ill. There are rules about absenteeism; if the employee violates them, that's when action is taken.

Form 2-4 is a simple interview schedule that would be appropriate to use when interviewing for a media clerk. Form 2-5 provides two job sample tests for a media clerk which, unlike interviews, are excellent predictors of job success. The Applicant Evaluation in Form 2-6 allows for anecdotal summation and recommendation. All three forms should be filed with the application form.

Do not fill in the Interview Schedule, Form 2-4, in the presence of the person seeking the position. To do so would be extremely disconcerting and may affect the quality of the answers given. Wait until the interview is concluded and the applicant has left. Then quickly jot down your recollections before doing anything else. The only question which can be recorded immediately is number 6. If there is a positive response, tell the person that you want to be sure you have noted all of his or her skills accurately, then read back your notes for verification.

Although you follow the schedule, don't begin the interview brusquely. Some friendly chatter is appropriate to put the person at ease. You need not and should not read every question, wait for a response, and then read out the next question. Try to give the interview the flow of natural conversation while still covering everything in sequence. You might look for the following types of responses to Form 2-4 questions:

2. The typical response might include good hours, good vacation time, and that the job is close to home. A somewhat better answer would be that the job offers the opportunity to work with children. An excellent answer might refer to the opportunity to improve personal skills in library use; to have the chance to work on a variety of tasks with many different types of equipment. Interviewees with children in the school district might want to become more familiar with the school their children attend.

3. Look for the interviewee's ability to make analogies. An example might be, "I keep an extensive recipe file" or "I have done specialized typing in a doctor's office."

4. Most people answer "no" to this question, but listen for someone willing to let you know of any reasonable reservations.

5. While some experience would be valuable, what you are really interested in is seeing if the interviewee seems interested in and comfortable about learning to work with machines.

6. This is an extension of Question 5.

7. If the answer is "yes," it is a definite plus since jobs in the library involve these activities.

8. You are looking for a flexible, self-assured, unflappable person, which this question should ascertain.

To give the job sample tests in Form 2-5, you need to make some preparations. For Test #1, Catalog Card Typing, have a perfect set of author, title, and subject cards for one book. Give the applicant enough time and several blank cards to allow for nervousness and some false starts. Walk away or turn to some other activity to relieve any tension. Do not comment specifically on the finished product. Just say, "Thank you very much. These will be fine" or any similar noncommittal statement. Take the typed cards and attach them to the job test form. Note the time. After the applicant has left, fill in the information on errors. Test #1 should take about 15 minutes with minor errors.

Job Sample Test #2, Catalog Card Filing, seems simple, but it is not. Use 25 cards that are ready to be filed. Be sure that several begin with the same first letter. Include a mixture of author, title, and subject cards. Check to be sure the applicant has followed directions and has not filed by author. It is not necessary that all peculiarities of library filing be observed since you did not explain all of them. The key here is to follow directions. Again, at the end of the test, don't comment on the quality of the work. Just record the time and thank the applicant for applying. Fill in the error information later. Test #2 should take 5 minutes or less.

NOTE: To adapt the job sample idea for a media aide, the test should include changing a lamp and/or laminating a picture. For the media technician, a job sample test would be to check a filmstrip projector that is not advancing the film properly and have the applicant describe the problem and propose a solution.

After the job sample tests have been completed, conclude the interview. Inquire if the applicant has any questions and answer as graciously and briefly as possible. Be sure to tell the person when you expect to reach a decision. A good general practice is to write to all applicants, letting them know when the position has been filled and thanking them for their time.

As a final step after the session is over, fill in the interview schedule, the error portion of the job sample tests, and the recommendation, Form 2-6. Put all papers together and route them to the proper authority, keeping a copy for your files.

FORMS FOR ORGANIZING VOLUNTEERS

Adult Volunteers (Forms 2-7—2-13)

Whether or not you have paid clerical help, adult volunteers are essential. Recruiting them is your responsibility, sometimes in cooperation with the P.T.A. Several methods may be used to encourage parents to volunteer. Probably the most direct method is to send a letter like the sample shown in Form 2-7 to the students' homes at the beginning of the school year. You can delegate the collation of responses to your volunteer chairperson from the previous year. Other simple ways of recruiting include posting a request for

Sayreville Public Schools
Harry S. Truman School

TAFT PLACE
PARLIN NEW JERSEY 08850

HENRY L OUNSMAN
SUPERINTENDENT
PETER I FLAND
PRINCIPAL

Telephone (201) 254 4400

Dear Parents:

Our library plays a significant role in your child's education, but we need your help.

The modern school media center is not only a place to borrow books, it also provides training in information-gathering skills, supports the curriculum, and maintains the audio-visual equipment and materials.

If you are willing to offer at least one half day per week, we would like you to join our active group of volunteers. No previous experience is necessary.

Become a part of your child's school world and make a contribution to his or her education.

                                        Sincerely,

                                        Hilda K. Weisburg

HKW:ldp   Hilda K. Weisburg
                                        Library Media Specialist

. . . .

Tear off this half and send it to school with your child. We will call you.

Name _____ Tel. # _____

                I am unable to volunteer at this time.
                I would like to volunteer. I prefer
                          A.M.   P.M.
_____MON   _____TUES.   _____WED.   _____THURS.   _____FRI.

'Affirmative Action Equal Opportunity Employer M F
'Nondiscrimination of the Handicapped'

FORM 2-7   Sample Form Letter Recruiting Volunteers

volunteers with a phone number to call on the bottom of the weekly lunch menus that are sent home, requesting volunteers at teas or orientations for new parents, and announcing your needs at the first P.T.A. meeting. To reach volunteers outside the school, try personally contacting senior citizens' clubs.

Once you have your adult volunteers with their requests for particular time slots, make up a schedule. Your volunteer chairperson can help. The basic Form 2-8 gives special attention to lunchtime coverage. You are more likely to be out of the media center at that time, and responsibilities can be misconstrued. A clear explanation of who is expected to cover the desk during overlapping time periods helps you avoid any problems.

On the schedule give telephone numbers as well as first and last names. The narrow column allows you to place a check mark next to the names of those persons who are experienced. If possible, it's advisable to pair inexperienced people with volunteers who are familiar with media center procedures.

Schedules can become extremely complex if volunteers report on alternate weeks or only for particular periods of time. In the latter case, try to have the time slots correspond with the school schedule. The more complex the schedule, the more necessary it becomes for everyone involved to have a copy.

Form 2-9 is for your personal convenience and should be kept at home. Additional copies may be placed in your plan book and filed at any other school in which you work. It allows ready alphabetical access to any volunteer at a moment's notice. This becomes necessary when you know you are going to be absent or late and specific instructions must be given.

Volunteers can be provided with a 4" × 6" card (Form 2-10) to enable them to contact others if they cannot report at their assigned time. The first people they are to call are those who work with them. Emergency substitutes are also listed. You can choose to put substitutes' names and phone numbers on schedule Form 2-8 and give each volunteer a copy of that instead.

Knowledge of certain basic procedures is required of everyone. As your volunteers change over the years, it is easy to lose track of who has been trained and what areas have been covered. A dated Volunteer Training Checklist, Form 2-11, is invaluable in organizing your support staff. Safety information has been placed first because it is often overlooked, but it is the most necessary information for volunteers to know. Lives can be involved and confidence in communication procedures is vital. Routine circulation and shelving procedures are itemized next. If there are other tasks in your media center, use this form as a guide, substituting your own routines.

Some volunteers may be skilled in certain tasks or may enjoy working on long-range projects. As you make these special assignments, keep track of who has taken on a particular responsibility. Form 2-12 provides a way of recording special task assignments. Although standard jobs are included, space is provided so that you can add many others, such as bulletin board work, art and display work, mending, covering books, or whatever else you require. A card file of volunteers engaged in special assignments, Form 2-13, can be kept. It is useful for considering personnel available for new projects. Knowing who types or who likes to do artwork helps you to become aware of the talent pool from which you can draw.

Many of the above forms can be used if you have paid clerical help. The training checklist, Form 2-11, and the special task assignment, Form 2-12, are particularly adaptable.

Student Volunteers (Forms 2-14—2-16)

Junior and senior high school media specialists have an additional source of help. Students in the upper grades are willing and able to work in the media center. As with all free help, there is a price to be paid.

First, you need to provide a place for interested students to sign up. The best location for Form 2-14 is in the media center. A poster nearby can announce this opportunity to students. Use the daily bulletin as an additional source to inform them where to find the sign-up sheet. Try to encourage some students to work before or after school, the times when adult volunteers are not usually available.

Scheduling students is a problem since they are only available at specific times. Use the school schedule as a basis for devising your own Student Volunteer Schedule Form 2-15. As with adults, try to cover the lunch periods. Give students and homeroom teachers a copy of this schedule.

PERIOD DAY	Monday	Tuesday	Wednesday	Thursday	Friday
Period 1 9:00–9:55	Mary Beth	Judy	Debbie	Jean	Frank
Period 2 9:55–10:45	Tom	Barbara	Andrew	Denise	Pat Susan
Period 3 10:51–11:41	Jean Ralph	Mike	Amy	Dan	Debbie
Lunch 1st Lunch 11:44–12:14	Amy	Pat	Mary Beth	Ted	Charlene
4 2nd Lunch 12:14–12:44	Denise	Susan	Judy	Andrew	Teresa
Period 3rd Lunch 12:44–1:14	Teresa	Ted	Ralph	Jean	Dean
Period 5 1:17–2:07	Dan	Bob Dan	Denise Barbara	Pat	Mike
Period 6 2:10–3:00	Frank	Charlene	Tom	Marie	Bob Mike

Week of: 9/28
Student Volunteer Schedule

FORM 2-15   Sample Student Volunteer Schedule

You are responsible for students when they are assigned to you. The Sign-In Sheet, Form 2-16, serves a double purpose. It allows a daily check of students who actually reported to the media center and it also shows which adult volunteers worked with them. Relationships can be fostered and you can use adults to supervise the students and to reduce your own load. This daily record may be a guide to determining special end-of-the-year awards.

Date: February 2   Day: Wednesday
Volunteer Sign-in Sheet

PERIOD	STUDENT VOLUNTEERS	ADULT VOLUNTEERS
Before Class	Amy	Mrs. Curtis
Period 1	Frank	Mrs. Curtis
Period 2	Frank	Mrs. Curtis
Period 3	Janet	Mr. Yarnell
1st Lunch	Rick	Mr. Yarnell
2nd Lunch	Teresa	Mr. Yarnell
3rd Lunch	Rhonda	Miss Francis
Period 5	Sandy	Miss Francis
Period 6	Dan	Miss Francis
After Class	Celeste	Miss Francis

FORM 2-16   Sample Sign-in Sheet

Library Media Needs Survey
Of Classroom Teachers

TEACHER	Grade/Subject	Room Number	Opening Unit

Library Media Needs Survey
Of Support Personnel

NAME	AREA	AIDE	SPECIAL NEEDS

FORM 2-2   Library Media Needs Survey of Support Personnel

INTERVIEW SCHEDULE

QUESTIONS:

1. Have you seen the complete job description for this
   position? (If not, hand it to the interviewee and allow
   ample time for it to be read.)

2. What most appeals to you about this position?

3. Have you done anything of a similar nature?

4. Is there any part of the job as described that you dislike
   or feel concerned about?

5. Have you any experience with school machines such as
   ditto? stencil? copiers?

6. Have you any experience with media equipment? Which ones
   —record players? cassette recorders? 16mm projectors?
   video? microform? (Include whatever is in your media
   center.)

7. Do you enjoy creating simple art work? Cutting and
   pasting? Do you think you have any special ability in
   this area?

8. In the course of the day, you will probably be
   interrupted many times while you are trying to complete
   work. You may also have planned to do one job, and, as you
   begin, be assigned to something entirely different. How
   do you think you would react?

Test #1—CATALOG CARD TYPING

Name _____ Date _____

Presentation: "Here are three typical catalog cards. You
                will notice that while there are similarities
                among the three cards, there are differences
                as well. These three cards are completely
                correct for media center use. Please type
                duplicates of all three cards as accurately as
                you can." (Give the interviewee a perfect set
                of author, title, and subject cards for a
                single book and several blank cards, and seat
                the interviewee at a typewriter.)

Time to complete task: _____

Number and type of errors: _____

Test #2—CATALOG CARD FILING

Name _____ Date _____

Presentation: "Here are 25 cards that need to be filed in the
                card catalog. They are to be filed
                alphabetically by the top line. If the first
                word on the line is "A," "An," or "The,"
                disregard it and file by the next word. Please
                put all of the cards in correct alphabetical
                sequence." (Give the interviewee 25 cards
                ready to be filed. Use a mixture of author,
                title, and subject cards.)

Time to complete test: _____

Number and type of errors: _____

FORM 2-5   Job Sample Tests

APPLICANT EVALUATION

Rate applicant on:

    SKILL POTENTIAL: (Use answers to questions and results of
                             Job Sample Test)

    PERSONALITY: (Consider friendliness, ability to express
                       self, general attitude)

_____

RECOMMENDATION:

    HIRE _____

    CONSIDER FOR FUTURE POSITION _____

    UNACCEPTABLE _____

Signature _____ Date _____

FORM 2-6   Applicant Evaluation

Library Volunteer Schedule

Day / Time	MONDAY		TUESDAY		WEDNESDAY		THURSDAY		FRIDAY	
A.M. VOLUNTEERS										
LUNCH COVERAGE										
P.M. VOLUNTEERS										

52

FORM 2-8   Library Volunteer Schedule

Date _____

Library Volunteer Record

Name of Volunteer	Telephone	Day/Time	Works with

```
+------------------------------------------------------------------+
|                                Day/Time works _____    |
|                                                                  |
| Name of Volunteer                                                |
+------------------------------------------------------------------+
|                                                                  |
| Works with _____     _____     |
|                    Name                      telephone           |
|                                                                  |
| and      _____        _____     |
|                    Name                      telephone           |
+------------------------------------------------------------------+
|                      EMERGENCY SUBSTITUTES                        |
+------------------------------------------------------------------+
|                                                                  |
| Name _____  Telephone _____    |
|                                                                  |
| Name _____  Telephone _____    |
|                                                                  |
| Library Telephone _____  |
+------------------------------------------------------------------+
```

FORM 2-10   Record for Volunteer Use

Date _____

Volunteer Training Checklist

TASK DESCRIPTION	Volunteers													
Safety Information														
Telephone														
Intercom														
Fire Drill Procedure														
Opening Routine														
Closing Routine														
Circulation Procedures														
Books—Students														
Books—Faculty														
Overnight														
Periodicals														
Vertical File														
Renewals														
Reserves														
Circulation Statistics														
A-V														
Shelving Procedures														
Books														
Periodicals														
A-V Materials														

Date _____

Volunteer Special Task Assignment

TASK DESCRIPTION	VOLUNTEER RESPONSIBLE
PROCESSING	
Books	
Paperbacks	
A-V	
Periodicals	
CATALOG CARDS—TYPING	
CATALOG CARDS—FILING	
SHELF LIST—FILING	
DISCARDS	
OVERDUES	
RELABELING	
VERTICAL FILE MAINTENANCE	
A-V MAINTENANCE	
Lamp Changing	
Cleaning	
Repair Records	
OTHER	

FORM 2-12   Volunteer Special Task Assignment

Volunteer Name

Telephone Number _____ **Day(s) Work** _____

Special Ability of Volunteer

Volunteer Name

Telephone Number _____ **Day(s) Work** _____

Special Ability of Volunteer

Volunteer Name

Telephone Number _____ **Day(s) Work** _____

Special Ability of Volunteer

FORM 2-13   Special Ability File Card

Student Sign-up Sheet

Student Name	Homeroom	Time Available		Available	
		Day	Period	Before	After

FORM 2-14   Student Sign-up Sheet

Student Volunteer Schedule

Week of: _____

PERIOD \ DAY	Monday	Tuesday	Wednesday	Thursday	Friday

FORM 2-15   Student Volunteer Schedule

Date _____   Day _____

VOLUNTEER SIGN-IN SHEET

Period	Student Volunteers	Adult Volunteers

FORM 2-16   Volunteer Sign-in Sheet

Section 3

Forms for Circulation Control

IT'S MY NEW PHYSICAL FITNESS PROGRAM—PAPER LIFTING.

With the physical and human resources under control, turn next to establishing satisfactory circulation procedures. Circulation plays a major role in media center service; it is the first level of contact people have with you and the media center. Good public relations here will have a positive effect on your other programs. The whole operation must allow for smooth daily functioning while at the same time causing you a minimum of extra work.

The media center generates an enormous amount of paper work and a great part of that emanates from circulation procedures. Although the tasks are clerical and should be accomplished by your staff, *you* must choose the forms to be used and set the tone that will be taken at the circulation desk.

The forms in this chapter govern the clerical interaction between the media center and its users, allowing student access, dealing with circulation problems such as overdues, reserves, lost books, and charge-out procedures, and recording the statistics of these operations. Once these forms are in use, your support staff, whether paid or volunteer, can perform many of the ongoing tasks under your supervision.

LIBRARY PASSES (FORMS 3-1—3-5)

Circulation begins with individuals coming to the media center. Most schools prefer to use some kind of student pass. A special library pass not only permits monitoring of hall traffic, but it also allows you to document media center use that may not involve the borrowing of materials.

Often secondary school media centers will want to keep a master list of students entering and exiting. Form 3-1 is a simple record to allow you to count the number of students who came into the media center on a given day.

Form 3-2 is the basic library pass. Form 3-3 allows you to maintain your records and to give students permission to return to class. Form 3-4 combines the two. An optional pass for junior and senior high school is Form 3-5. It is more formal and shows individual students' use over a period of time.

FORMS FOR CHARGE-OUT PROCEDURES

Book Cards (Forms 3-6—3-9)

Book cards come in a variety of colors, weights, and formats. You naturally would not make your own book cards; it is not "cost-effective" to do so. On the other hand, you must make an intelligent decision about which type of book card is the best choice for your media center. The many options prove there is no single answer that is correct for all situations.

All variations described refer to those cards that library supply houses call "school library book cards." If you use a charging system other than stamping by hand, the choices are different, particularly those involving format. Although you will select cards compatible with your charging system, some of the following considerations will still apply.

• *Weight:* First choose the card weight you want. Medium weight and lightweight stock are generally offered, with lightweight cards costing less. Book cards do not need the capacity for a long shelf life. As soon as the spaces are filled, a new card is used. Lightweight cards can stand up to normal wear. Their disadvantages lie mainly in that they feel thin, bend easily, and have a tendency—particularly when new—to stick to each other, causing minor annoyances when the cards are counted. The card choice you make depends on how closely you must figure pennies and whether you feel the drawbacks of lightweight cards are serious. Try experimenting with both types if you are not sure which you prefer.

• *Color:* Colors should be limited to prevent the development of a rainbow effect in the file, which complicates rather than simplifies circulation procedures. Although it is possible to use different colors for paperbacks, periodicals, media, and vertical file and overnight materials, try to combine less heavily circulating types so that no more than four colors are used.

• *Format:* Further variations are offered by format. You must look closely at catalog illustrations to see this difference since the supply houses do not usually describe the cards, they merely assign different order numbers to different formats. The simplest option is between unlined cards (Forms 3-6 and 3-8) and those with lines ruled for author and title (Forms 3-7 and 3-9). If you do not have a typewriter available and must letter the information, cards with lines are the better choice. Otherwise you are best served by a blank top, as in Forms 3-6 and 3-8. It is not worth the effort to align the cards in the typewriter, and too often the typed information is entered too far above the line or through the line itself.

The last format problem is how the columns are to be headed. "Date Loaned" (Form 3-7) is easiest for the student. "Date Due" (Form 3-6) is easiest for the media specialist since cards are normally filed behind the due date. Yet, when you deal with children, you quickly become aware that they are confused by a date one or two weeks in the future. Students do adapt when necessary, but you have another choice. The card can be stamped with the date on which the book was loaned, and a prestamped due-date card can be put into the book pocket. The format in Form 3-9, which has a left-hand column for "Date Loaned" and a right-hand column for "Date Due," functions well only when students have library cards. The card number is filled in under "Borrower's Name." If it becomes necessary to send an overdue notice, you check the numerical listing of card holders to locate the borrower's home room. When you don't use library cards, this card doesn't work well. The format you choose should be the one that makes the most sense to you.

A word about library cards: The purpose of a library card is to permit you to know who borrowed material and where they can be reached if necessary. In small schools, the child's name and room number are sufficient and there is no need for cards. In large schools, or where illegible handwriting has become a major problem, library cards are advisable. However, before you start the system, remember that it will add to the clerical load. Two-way records must be kept—an alphabetical list of students with library card numbers, and a numerical list of card numbers with students' names and current room numbers.

Periodical Charge Card (Form 3-10)

The format for periodical charge cards is awkward to use in most media centers. There is one line at the top for the title of the periodical. The left-hand column is headed "Date of Magazine," (Form 3-10). Most library media specialists find it impractical to record different issue dates on one card. While a periodical card is rarely filled before the magazine is discarded, if you are very penny-conscious it is simpler to type a new label or to erase the issue date on an old card and replace it with the date of the current issue than to enter the new issue date in a left-hand column and have no place to record the due date. The majority of library media specialists choose to treat periodical cards as book cards and to use that left-hand column for stamping the due date or date loaned. Many media centers do not purchase periodical cards at all and just use regular book cards, possibly in a different color. If you want the cherry color, however, you may have to purchase periodical cards because that shade is not generally available in other formats.

BOOK POCKETS

Whether you choose gummed or ungummed, imprinted or plain, the special options for book pockets are a matter of budget, size of staff, and time available. A media specialist without any clerical help should buy imprinted, gummed pockets to minimize the already excessive amount of time spent on clerical work. Other decisions are up to you.

Generally the high-backed pocket favored by commercial processors serves most needs. You may want a small supply of pockets that don't have space for stamping the due date. These are handy for processing small-sized picture books. You can paste in a miniature due-date slip (the type used to cover the filled portion on a book pocket) where it fits conveniently.

OTHER CIRCULATION FORMS (FORMS 3-11—3-20)

Throughout the year you receive your magazines weekly, monthly, or bi-monthly. For checking in individual titles, periodical record cards are available from library supply houses. Although you might normally check off each card as part of processing operations (when cards and pockets are inserted), you will find it extremely helpful to have a master periodical chart (Form 3-11) which shows the up-to-the-minute state of all of your periodical holdings. Anyone who sorts the mail should record on the master chart the date the magazine arrives. In this way you will develop the "publishing history" of each periodical. Since each publication has a different pattern of mailing—one month in advance of issue date, during the month of issue date, etc.—you will know whether an issue is late in arriving or has been lost in the mail. You can then take steps immediately to notify the supplier of the problem.

Form 3-11 can be used in several ways. Depending on the size of your collection and your physical facilities, either enlarge it to large posterboard size by using the overhead projector or make several photocopies of the form to keep in a notebook, in a file folder, or on your office wall for easy viewing.

Teacher sign-out of software can be handled in one of three ways. A method that closely follows the procedure for circulating print material is to simply use a book card, possibly in a different color. Be sure to prepare cards for each component in a set in case teachers want to sign out only one part. A very simple operation for a small school with little clerical help is Form 3-12, a Teacher Software Sign-Out Sheet. Arrange the forms either alphabetically by the teachers' names or sequentially by grade. Keep them in a loose-leaf notebook at the circulation desk for teachers to sign out and also to see who has materials that they need. Form 3-13 is to be put on cards. It is a highly complex method for a large system having a master file and heavy interschool loans. Use this form only when there is an a-v coordinator and lots of help. The numbers along the top represent the months of the year. Metal flags are clipped to the number corresponding to the month the software was borrowed to indicate how long the material has been out.

If software circulates to students, use the book-card system described above. For media centers that do not permit circulation but that allow student access to software within the building, a Student Software Sign-Out Sheet (Form 3-14) is usable.

Keeping control of hardware is an extremely trying task. No system is perfect because teachers exchange equipment frequently without notifying the media center. Occasionally an emergency routing of equipment is not recorded. Snags are to be expected, no matter how organized you are. To minimize problems, try using two or three systems in concert. Your records will usually be accurate on at least one of them. Adapt these forms to meet your needs, but make sure that you have access by three routes—equipment, teacher, and grade level/subject area/physical location.

Form 3-15 allows you to see where each piece of equipment is located, either with a teacher, in the media center, or out for repair. Recreate your own holdings on a posterboard. As shown on sample Form 3-15, give the code or number for each piece of equipment, and, if you desire, its serial number. Cover the posterboard with clear Con-Tact paper. Use a washable transparency marker to fill in current usage. (All equipment with no location or notation next to it remains in the media center.) You can easily rub it out when change is necessary. If you do not have the space for such a large board, use a standard-size page and record the location in pencil.

Form 3-16 gives you two types of information. Reading across indicates which teachers have which equipment. Reading down gives the location of hardware. Again, you can cover this form with Con-Tact paper. Form 3-16 refers to equipment assigned to a-v storage areas. Use Forms 3-17 and 3-18 for equipment within these areas. Form 3-17 tells teachers which equipment is available in their area. Note which equipment is out for repair or is temporarily assigned elsewhere. Form 3-18 allows teachers to reserve equipment in their area.

An Equipment Control Board (Form 3-19) combines area and equipment in a fashion similar to Form 3-16. As shown in the sample, you use one-inch posterboard squares for each piece of hardware. Color-coded push pins indicate

FORM 3-15   Sample Hardware Distribution Chart by Equipment

FORM 3-19   Sample Equipment Control Board

the type of equipment, such as blue for overhead projectors and white for record players. Room numbers are within particular team assignments.

If you receive 16mm films on a regular basis from a film library, use
Form 3-20 to help teachers avoid conflicts when scheduling. When the films
arrive, number them and list their running times. Post this information next
to the schedule. Note that your week begins with the day the film is delivered.

FORM 3-20   Sample Film Schedule

RESERVE FORMS (FORMS 3-21—3-23)

When students wish to reserve a book, use Form 3-21. Scrap catalog cards are perfect for the job. Ruled lines are optional. Record the author, title, and call number on top and have students sign the card. In the left-hand column, enter the date you send the reserve notice. In media centers with heavy reserves, you will need a separate card for each request. In this case, you might prefer to use paper copies of the blank form provided at the end of this section. Date requests to keep them in order. When the book is returned, notify students with either Form 3-22 or 3-23.

FIC
CLE

Cleaver, Vera
Ellen Grae

Notified	Name	Room
3/16	Joel Marks	15

FORM 3-21   Sample Reserve Form

OVERDUE NOTICES (FORMS 3-24—3-33)

When material is kept beyond the due date, the borrower must be notified. Form 3-24 is a Combined Overdue/Reserve Notice, which minimizes the number of forms necessary. Another basic type of notice is Form 3-25. If you prefer a variety, use Forms 3-26, 3-27, and 3-28 in succession. The different formats remind students that time is passing. Form 3-29 is helpful if you allow overnight circulation of materials. For items excessively overdue, you may wish to communicate with parents (see Section 8). Teacher cooperation can be obtained by using Form 3-30.

Teachers are only human and sometimes they, too, have overdue materials. If possible, talk to them face to face if a problem exists. In a large system where this might be difficult, use Forms 3-31 or 3-32. Be aware that Form 3-32 is a little sharper and should be used with caution. If it is your school's policy to charge fines and you are required to keep a record, Form 3-33 can be used for an entire school year.

LOST BOOKS FORMS (FORMS 3-34, 3-35)

To keep track of money received for lost books use Form 3-34. Give students a receipt for their own records using Form 3-35.

INTERLIBRARY LOAN FORM (FORM 3-36)

Schools that are part of a network will use commercially produced interlibrary loan forms. However, if you have an informal arrangement with the other schools in your district and would like to document the extent of your services, use Form 3-36. The requesting library completes the majority of the form. The library fulfilling the request will keep the top half for its records and return the bottom half with the material requested. This allows each to keep a permanent record of the transaction.

STATISTICS RECORDS (FORMS 3-37—3-41)

Circulation statistics should be kept whether or not you are required to submit them. Tailor your statistical record to your system by having the high school graphic arts department print the forms according to your design. Turn the daily printed form (Form 3-37), into a pad using pad paste. Making your own forms allows you to arrange your cumulative statistics in the same sequence as your daily ones. (Commercial forms never seem to agree.)

Transfer your daily statistics, done in pencil, to a monthly record (Form 3-38). To record staff and student loans simultaneously, use a slash mark in each box with student figures coming first. An annual cumulation (Form 3-39) gives an instant view of the year and is excellent for submission to your supervisor as part of your annual report (see Section 7). Additions to and discards from the collection are noted on Forms 3-40 and 3-41. These, too, can be photocopied and attached to your annual report.

Date _____

STUDENT SIGN-IN SHEET

Student Name	From Rm. Number	Time In	Time Out

FORM 3-1   Student Sign-In Sheet

LIBRARY PASS

Room _____ Date _____

Student _____

Time out _____

Teacher Signature _____

LIBRARY PASS

Room _____ Date _____

Student _____

Time out _____

Teacher Signature _____

LIBRARY PASS

Room _____ Date _____

Student _____

Time out _____

Teacher Signature _____

LIBRARY PASS

Room _____ Date _____

Student _____

Time out _____

Teacher Signature _____

LIBRARY PASS

Room _____ Date _____

Student _____

Time out _____

Teacher Signature _____

LIBRARY PASS

Room _____ Date _____

Student _____

Time out _____

Teacher Signature _____

FORM 3-2   Library Pass

RETURN PASS

Student _____

Date _____

Time out _____

Library Signature _____

RETURN PASS

Student _____

Date _____

Time out _____

Library Signature _____

RETURN PASS

Student _____

Date _____

Time out _____

Library Signature _____

RETURN PASS

Student _____

Date _____

Time out _____

Library Signature _____

RETURN PASS

Student _____

Date _____

Time out _____

Library Signature _____

RETURN PASS

Student _____

Date _____

Time out _____

Library Signature _____

LIBRARY/CLASS PASS

Room _____ Date _____

Student _____

Time left class _____ Time left library _____

Teacher Signature _____

Library Signature _____

LIBRARY/CLASS PASS

Room _____ Date _____

Student _____

Time left class _____ Time left library _____

Teacher Signature _____

Library Signature _____

LIBRARY/CLASS PASS

Room _____ Date _____

Student _____

Time left class _____ Time left library _____

Teacher Signature _____

Library Signature _____

LIBRARY/CLASS PASS

Room _____ Date _____

Student _____

Time left class _____ Time left library _____

Teacher Signature _____

Library Signature _____

LIBRARY/CLASS PASS

Room _____ Date _____

Student _____

Time left class _____ Time left library _____

Teacher Signature _____

Library Signature _____

LIBRARY/CLASS PASS

Room _____ Date _____

Student _____

Time left class _____ Time left library _____

Teacher Signature _____

Library Signature _____

FORM 3-4   Library/Class Pass

LIBRARY RECORD PASS

Student _____

Room Number _____ Teacher _____

Date	Time out	Teacher	Time out	Media Specialist

LIBRARY RECORD PASS

Student _____

Room Number _____ Teacher _____

Date	Time out	Teacher	Time out	Media Specialist

FORM 3-5   Library Record Pass

AUTHOR			
TITLE			
Date Loaned	Borrower's Name		Room Number

FORM 3-7   Book Card (date loaned, lined)

Date Due	Borrower's Name	

FORM 3-6   Book Card (date due, unlined)

AUTHOR			
TITLE			
Date Loaned	Borrower's Name		Date Due

FORM 3-9 Book Card (date loaned/date due, lined)

Date	Issued To

FORM 3-8 Book Card (unlined)

Date of Magazine	Borrower's Name	Due

FORM 3-10   Periodical Charge Card

MASTER PERIODICAL CHART
Year _____

Periodical Name	September	October	November	December	January	February	March	April	May	June	July	August

FORM 3-11 Master Periodical Chart

TEACHER _____

TYPE	CALL NUMBER	TITLE	DATE OUT	DATE IN

FORM 3-12   Teacher Software Sign-out Sheet

1	2	3	4	5	6	7	8	9	10	11	12

TITLE: _____

SERIES/SET TITLE: _____

Level: _____

Subj. Areas: _____

CONTENTS: _____

PRODUCER: _____

CATALOG NUMBER: _____

NAME	DATE OUT	DATE IN	SCHOOL

NAME	DATE OUT	DATE IN	SCHOOL

FORM 3-13   Teacher Software Sign-out Card

STUDENT SOFTWARE SIGN-OUT SHEET

Date _____

STUDENT NAME	ROOM NUMBER	CALL NUMBER	TITLE	TIME OUT	TIME IN

FORM 3-14   Student Software Sign-out Sheet

Hardware Distribution Chart by Equipment

Filmstrip Projectors (FS)												
Previewers (FP)												
Cassette Recorders (CR)												
Cassette Playbacks (PC)												
Listening Stations (LS)												
Overhead Projectors (OP)												
Opaque Projectors (Q)												
Record Players (R)												
16mm Projectors (16)												
8mm Projectors (8)												
Loop Projectors (8L)												
Cameras (X)												
Slide Projectors (SL)												

FORM 3-15   Hardware Distribution Chart by Equipment

84

TEACHERS	EQUIPMENT	8mm & 16mm Projectors	Overhead & Opaque Projectors	Filmstrip Projector & Previewers	Slide Projectors	Record Players	Cassette & Reel-to-Reel Players	Listening Stations	Video Equipment	Cameras	Other
A-V Storage Area 1											
A-V Storage Area 2											
A-V Storage Area 3											
Other Area											
Repair											

FORM 3-16   Hardware Distribution Chart by Teacher

Area Hardware Assignment

THE FOLLOWING EQUIPMENT IS ASSIGNED TO THIS AREA. IF YOU CANNOT ACCOUNT FOR THE LOCATION OF A PIECE OF EQUIPMENT ON THIS LIST, PLEASE INFORM _____.

EQUIPMENT AND CODE	SPECIAL NOTES ON CURRENT STATUS

FORM 3-17   Area Hardware Assignment Sheet

Equipment Reserve
Area _____

Equipment Type (Code Number)	Reserved By	Date	Time	Returned (Initial)

FILM SCHEDULE

Week of _____

Two people may sign for each time slot, but please indicate NUMBER of film

TIME	FLOOR	Monday	Tuesday	Wednesday	Thursday	Friday

FORM 3-20   Film Schedule

Notified	Name	Room	Notified	Name	Room	Notified	Name	Room

FORM 3-21   Reserve Form

Room Number _____ Date _____

_____, please come to the

(Name)

media center. _____

(Title)

that you reserved is waiting for you.

Thank you!

Room Number _____ Date _____

_____, please come to the

(Name)

media center. _____

(Title)

that you reserved is waiting for you.

Thank you!

Room Number _____ Date _____

_____, please come to the

(Name)

media center. _____

(Title)

that you reserved is waiting for you.

Thank you!

Room Number _____ Date _____

_____, please come to the

(Name)

media center. _____

(Title)

that you reserved is waiting for you.

Thank you!

Room Number _____ Date _____

_____, please come to the

(Name)

media center. _____

(Title)

that you reserved is waiting for you.

Thank you!

Room Number _____ Date _____

_____, please come to the

(Name)

media center. _____

(Title)

that you reserved is waiting for you.

Thank you!

FORM 3-22   Reserve Notice Form with Owl

To _____
(Name)

Room Number _____ Date _____

We are holding _____
(Title)

which you reserved. Please come to the media center before _____

Thank you!

To _____
(Name)

Room Number _____ Date _____

We are holding _____
(Title)

which you reserved. Please come to the media center before _____

Thank you!

To _____
(Name)

Room Number _____ Date _____

We are holding _____
(Title)

which you reserved. Please come to the media center before _____

Thank you!

To _____
(Name)

Room Number _____ Date _____

We are holding _____
(Title)

which you reserved. Please come to the media center before _____

Thank you!

To _____
(Name)

Room Number _____ Date _____

We are holding _____
(Title)

which you reserved. Please come to the media center before _____

Thank you!

To _____
(Name)

Room Number _____ Date _____

We are holding _____
(Title)

which you reserved. Please come to the media center before _____

Thank you!

FORM 3-23   Reserve Notice Form

Room Number _____ **Date** _____

Student _____

Please come to the media center about the following:
Call Number   Title

_____

_____ Overdue since _____

_____ 1st notice _____ 2nd notice _____ 3rd notice

_____ Being held or reserve for you until _____

Thank you. _____
signature

Room Number _____ **Date** _____

Student _____

Please come to the media center about the following:
Call Number   Title

_____

_____ Overdue since _____

_____ 1st notice _____ 2nd notice _____ 3rd notice

_____ Being held on reserve for you until _____

Thank you. _____
signature

Room Number _____ **Date** _____

Student _____

Please come to the media center about the following:
Call Number   Title

_____

_____ Overdue since _____

_____ 1st notice _____ 2nd notice _____ 3rd notice

_____ Being held on reserve for you until _____

Thank you. _____
signature

Room Number _____ **Date** _____

Student _____

Please come to the media center about the following:
Call Number   Title

_____

_____ Overdue since _____

_____ 1st notice _____ 2nd notice _____ 3rd notice

_____ Being held on reserve for you until _____

Thank you. _____
signature

FORM 3-24   Combined Overdue/Reserve Notice

Room _____ **Date** _____

Student _____

Please return the following:

Call Number _____ Title _____

_____

Overdue since _____ ☐ 1st notice ☐ 2nd notice ☐ 3rd notice

Thank you _____
signature

FORM 3-25 Overdue Notice

oh! oh! **FIRST NOTICE**

Room_____ Date_____

Student_____

The following is now overdue:

YOU FORGOT!

Call Number _____ Title _____

_____

_____

Please return   Thank You!

oh! oh! **FIRST NOTICE**

Room_____ Date_____

Student_____

The following is now overdue:

YOU FORGOT!

Call Number _____ Title _____

_____

_____

Please return   Thank You!

oh! oh! **FIRST NOTICE**

Room_____ Date_____

Student_____

The following is now overdue:

YOU FORGOT!

Call Number _____ Title _____

_____

_____

Please return   Thank You!

oh! oh! **FIRST NOTICE**

Room_____ Date_____

Student_____

The following is now overdue:

YOU FORGOT!

Call Number _____ Title _____

_____

_____

Please return   Thank You!

FORM 3-26   First Notice

SECOND NOTICE

Room _____ Date _____

Student _____

Return the following as soon as possible

Call number   Title

_____

_____

_____

SECOND NOTICE

Room _____ Date _____

Student _____

Return the following as soon as possible

Call number   Title

_____

_____

_____

SECOND NOTICE

Room _____ Date _____

Student _____

Return the following as soon as possible

Call number   Title

_____

_____

_____

SECOND NOTICE

Room _____ Date _____

Student _____

Return the following as soon as possible

Call number   Title

_____

_____

_____

FORM 3-27   Second Notice

FORM 3-28   Third Notice

URGENT

Room _____

Date _____

Student _____

Overnight material now overdue

_____
_____
_____
_____

URGENT

Room _____

Date _____

Student _____

Overnight material now overdue

_____
_____
_____
_____

URGENT

Room _____

Date _____

Student _____

Overnight material now overdue

_____
_____
_____
_____

URGENT

Room _____

Date _____

Student _____

Overnight material now overdue

_____
_____
_____
_____

FORM 3-29   Overnight Overdue Form

A MEMO FROM THE MEDIA CENTER

Date _____

_____

Please remind the following students to return the overdue material listed below.

Thank you,

STUDENT	CALL #	TITLE	DATE DUE

FORM 3-30   Teacher Notice of Student Overdues

A MEMO FROM THE MEDIA CENTER

Date _____

_____

   According to our records you have the following material(s). Please check to make sure they are still in your possession as you have had them for quite some time. Please return anything you are no longer using.

Thank you,

Date _____

_____

Our records indicate you have had the following media center material(s) for an extended period of time. Please return them as soon as possible because there are requests for this material on file.

Thank you,

Payments Received—Fines

Week of	Total Fines		Signature	Week of	Total Fines		Signature

Payments Received—Lost Books

Date	Received From	Room	Title	Amount	

FORM 3-34   Payments Received Record—Lost Books

RECEIPT

Received from _____

Amount _____ Date _____

In payment for _____

_____

Signed _____

RECEIPT

Received from _____

Amount _____ Date _____

In payment for _____

_____

Signed _____

RECEIPT

Received from _____

Amount _____ Date _____

In payment for _____

_____

Signed _____

RECEIPT

Received from _____

Amount _____ Date _____

In payment for _____

_____

Signed _____

RECEIPT

Received from _____

Amount _____ Date _____

In payment for _____

_____

Signed _____

RECEIPT

Received from _____

Amount _____ Date _____

In payment for _____

_____

Signed _____

FORM 3-35   Receipt

INTERLIBRARY LOAN—REQUEST

Request From _____ Date _____

Call Number _____ Author _____

Title _____

Date Sent _____ Date Returned _____

. . . .

INTERLIBRARY LOAN—RECEIPT

On Loan From _____ Requested By _____

Call Number _____ Author _____

Title _____

Date Received _____ Date Returned _____

INTERLIBRARY LOAN—REQUEST

Request From _____ Date _____

Call Number _____ Author _____

Title _____

Date Sent _____ Date Returned _____

. . . .

INTERLIBRARY LOAN—RECEIPT

On Loan From _____ Requested By _____

Call Number _____ Author _____

Title _____

Date Received _____ Date Returned _____

FORM 3-36   Interlibrary Loan Request/Receipt

DATE _____		
Classification Nos.	**Student**	**Staff**
000		
100		
200		
300		
400		
500		
600		
700		
800		
900		
B		
Fiction		
Nonprint		
Periodicals		
Vertical File		
Total		

Signature _____

DATE _____		
Classification Nos.	**Student**	**Staff**
000		
100		
200		
300		
400		
500		
600		
700		
800		
900		
B		
Fiction		
Nonprint		
Periodicals		
Vertical File		
Total		

Signature _____

FORM 3-37   Daily Circulation Statistics

MONTH _____

	000	100	200	300	400	500	600	700	800	900	B	Fiction	Nonprint	Periodical	Vert. File	Total
1																
2																
3																
4																
5																
6																
7																
8																
9																
10																
11																
12																
13																
14																
15																
16																
17																
18																
19																
20																
21																
22																
23																
24																
25																
26																
27																
28																
29																
30																
31																
TOTAL																

FORM 3-38   Monthly Circulation Statistics

Annual Circulation Statistics   19____

	000	100	200	300	400	500	600	700	800	900	B	Fiction	Nonprint	Periodicals	Vert. File	TOTAL
September																
October																
November																
December																
January																
February																
March																
April																
May																
June																
TOTAL																

FORM 3-39   Annual Circulation Statistics

Additions 19____—19____

	000	100	200	300	400	500	600	700	800	900	B	Fiction	Nonprint	Periodicals	Vert. File	TOTAL
September																
October																
November																
December																
January																
February																
March																
April																
May																
June																
TOTAL																

FORM 3-40 Record of Additions to Collection

Discards 19___—19___

	000	100	200	300	400	500	600	700	800	900	B	Fiction	Paperback	Nonprint	Vert. File	TOTAL
September																
October																
November																
December																
January																
February																
March																
April																
May																
June																
TOTAL																

FORM 3-41   Record of Discards from Collection

Section 4

Forms for Technical Services

WELL, EVERYONE THINKS THE BOOKS GET
ON THE SHELVES BY MAGIC.

Technical services include the selection, acquisition, and maintenance of the collection. This behind-the-scenes activity requires careful management to allow the media center to function smoothly. Unlike other areas, such as circulation control, most of the burdens of technical services fall on the shoulders of the library media specialist. Under optimal conditions, your clients are generally unaware of the existence of this operation, although it is one of the most critical areas of your professional responsibility. The only time technical services are noticed by people outside the media center is when the processes break down and you fail to deliver needed items. The only kind of awareness is negative, so you must work to keep the operation running smoothly.

Since the collection is the backbone of the media center, the degree of service you can give depends on the quality and accessibility of the collection. Forms for ordering, evaluating, and maintaining materials and hardware, as well as for providing maximum access to the collection through the card catalog and shelf list, are included in this chapter.

BOOK ORDER CARD (FORM 4-1)

Acquisition is the first job in technical services. As you read reviews, see books on exhibition, or receive requests, fill out one order card per title. Scrap catalog cards work well for this purpose. You can use commercial order cards or Form 4-1, which is designed to meet the needs of a typical school media center. The box in the upper left-hand corner accommodates not only the number of copies, but also the call number if it is given. Classification numbers will act as a guide when you decide on which items to cut from your order.

CATALOG CARDS (FORMS 4-2—4-5)

Whenever you purchase unprocessed books, you must see that catalog cards are prepared. A clerk or volunteer must handle this job because it is far too time-consuming to take up your professional time. You can type each book's main entry card as a guide, but your staff must be instructed in how to complete the operation. Form 4-2 shows the author or main entry card, Form 4-3 shows the title card, and Form 4-4 shows the subject card. If the subject entry contains a dash, be sure that the typist understands that a double dash is needed to differentiate it from a hyphen. Because preparing catalog cards is an exacting procedure, your typist should have Forms 4-2, 4-3, 4-4, and 4-5 readily available as guides at all times.

The shelf list card, Form 4-5, requires special attention. It never includes annotations. You need this space to record the date the book was purchased, the source, the price, and copy or accession number. This card contains your complete record of purchases and expenditures for that particular title. Even though you may purchase three copies of a book, you have only *one* shelf list card on which all the information is recorded.

JOBBER SPECIFICATIONS

If you purchase books through a jobber (a company that handles books from many different publishers), you must choose from a list of specifications exactly how you want your books to be processed. Do you want just catalog cards, or plastic jackets and cards and pockets as well? Do you want the card to read FIC or just F? How do you want your biographies listed? Do you want one letter of the author's last name, or two, or three?

Despite these choices, there are limits to the amount of individualization offered. Easy and picture books are not distinguished from each other. If you prefer a separate classification for each, request that books be sent without any call number and type in your own. If the jobber offers extra catalog cards, by all means take them. You can use the cards for additional subject headings if you choose, but most often you will find them handy to use as scrap cards. Each jobber has his own form for specifications. Be sure to keep a copy of the specifications you sent to the jobber for your files.

BOOK PROCESSING FLOW CHART (FORM 4-6)

Whether you do in-house cataloging or buy your books from a jobber, you still need to prepare them for circulation. Multiple steps are involved and once again the operation should be mainly handled by the clerical staff. A flow chart is a visual representation of the steps involved. Form 4-6 is one example. Note that arrows indicate the flow of work. Rectangles show a process. Diamonds are used to show a decision that must be answered either yes or no. Use the form as a guide in preparing your own flow chart to simplify your staff training.

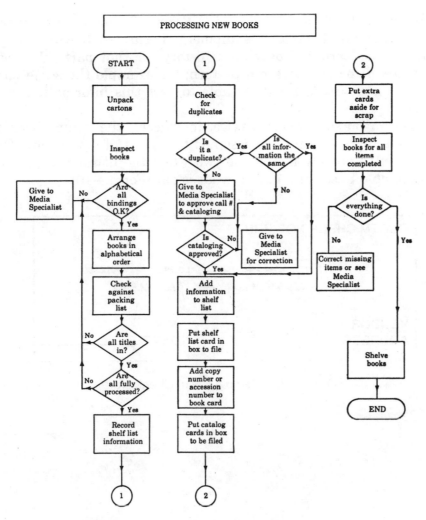

FORM 4-6   Sample Book Processing Flow Chart

EQUIPMENT EVALUATION (FORM 4-7)

Today, acquisition includes the purchase of audio-visual materials. Software purchasing is discussed in Section 6 (see Form 6-13). When you consider a hardware purchase, you will generally be doing a comparative analysis among several different brands. Form 4-7 allows you to keep a record of your findings and document the reason that caused you to make your final decision.

HARDWARE REPAIR AND MAINTENANCE FORMS (FORMS 4-8—4-10)

Additional behind-the-scenes responsibilities with hardware include repair and maintenance. You should have a Purchase Record Card for each piece of equipment, Form 4-8. Filed behind Form 4-8 should be a separate repair record card for each piece of equipment, Form 4-9. Record each breakdown on the proper card and develop a history for that particular machine. Very often you will be able to see a pattern; for example the same part malfunctions over the years. You will be able to pass this information on to the repair service.

    If you use an outside repair service, include on the claim check that is left with you the number you have assigned to a piece of equipment. This procedure helps you to quickly match the two when the equipment is returned, and you will be able to see at a glance what is out (Form 4-10).

CLAIM CHECK NO. 3397

16/3 — Does not hold frames properly — flutters

VENDOR NAME
ADDRESS   DATE _____

FORM 4-10   Sample Claim Check Note

NUMBER of COPIES	AUTHOR		
	TITLE		
PUBLISHER	ISBN		PRICE
COMMENT			

SOURCE _____ DATE _____ PAGE _____

DATE _____ PAGE _____

FORM 4-1   Book Order Card

FIC   Fleischman, Sid
FLE   McBroom tells the truth. Norton,
          c1966.
                47 p. illus.

          A farm where beans can be planted and harvested in one
          hour can start a lot of rumors, and McBroom sets down
          the "facts."

          1. Gardening—Fiction   I. Title

FORM 4-2   Author Card

FIC
FLE

McBroom tells the truth
Fleischman, Sid
    McBroom tells the truth. Norton,
c1966.
    47 p. illus.

A farm where beans can be planted and harvested in one hour can start a lot of rumors, and McBroom sets down the "facts."

1. Gardening—Fiction   I. Title

FORM 4-3   Title Card

FIC
FLE

GARDENING—FICTION
Fleischman, Sid
    McBroom tells the truth. Norton,
c1966.
    47 p. illus.

A farm where beans can be planted and harvested in one hour can start a lot of rumors, and McBroom sets down the "facts."

1. Gardening—Fiction   I. Title

FORM 4-4   Subject Card

FIC
FLE

Fleischman, Sid
    McBroom tells the truth. Norton,
c1966.
    47 p. illus.

5/70 B&T   5-12.407   4.95
3/72 Norton   5-15.021   5.95

1. Gardening—Fiction   I. Title

FORM 4-5   Shelf List Card

EQUIPMENT EVALUATION—Purchase Consideration

TYPE OF EQUIPMENT	PURCHASE ORDER NUMBER	
REQUESTED BY	DATE ORDERED	BID PRICE
REASON FOR REQUEST	MANUFACTURER AND MODEL RECOMMENDED	
	DEALER NAME	
	ADDRESS	

MANUFACTURER AND MODEL EVALUATED (√BOX IF USED IN DISTRICT)	COST QUOTED
1. ☐ _____	1. _____
2. ☐ _____	2. _____
3. ☐ _____	3. _____

MANUFACTURER AND MODEL ANALYSIS—USE REVERSE SIDE FOR ADDITIONAL COMMENTS

1 COMPATIBLE WITH DISTRICT EQUIPMENT? YES ☐ NO ☐	REPAIR RECORD IN DISTRICT SCHOOLS GOOD ☐ FAIR ☐ POOR ☐ DOES NOT APPLY ☐
IF NO—EXPLAIN	EVALUATIONS BY TRADE PUBLICATIONS—OTHER SOURCES
SPECIAL FEATURES—GIVE SOURCE	UNUSUAL OPERATING COSTS IF ANY
SPECIAL DEFECTS—GIVE SOURCE	

2 COMPATIBLE WITH DISTRICT EQUIPMENT? YES ☐ NO ☐	REPAIR RECORD IN DISTRICT SCHOOLS GOOD ☐ FAIR ☐ POOR ☐ DOES NOT APPLY ☐
IF NO—EXPLAIN	EVALUATIONS BY TRADE PUBLICATIONS—OTHER SOURCES
SPECIAL FEATURES—GIVE SOURCE	UNUSUAL OPERATING COSTS IF ANY
SPECIAL DEFECTS—GIVE SOURCE	

3 COMPATIBLE WITH DISTRICT EQUIPMENT? YES ☐ NO ☐	REPAIR RECORD IN DISTRICT SCHOOLS GOOD ☐ FAIR ☐ POOR ☐ DOES NOT APPLY ☐
IF NO—EXPLAIN	EVALUATIONS BY TRADE PUBLICATIONS—OTHER SOURCES
SPECIAL FEATURES—GIVE SOURCE	UNUSUAL OPERATING COSTS—IF ANY
SPECIAL DEFECTS—GIVE SOURCE	

FORM 4-7   Equipment Evaluation Form

CODE _____

EQUIPMENT TYPE _____

MAKE _____   MODEL _____

LAMP _____   NUMBER OWNED _____

NUMBER	DATE PURCHASED	P.O. #	NUMBER	DATE PURCHASED	P.O. #

FORM 4-8   Purchase Record Card

CODE _____   SERIAL NUMBER _____

DATE OUT	CLAIM CHECK NO.	REASON FOR REPAIR	DATE IN

FORM 4-9   Individual Equipment Repair Record

Section 5

Forms for Managing Library Programs

MEDIA CENTER

WELCOME

I HOPE I'M NOT BEING TOO SUBTLE.

A media center is ultimately judged by its programs. Everything else exists to allow these services to run effectively. Programs cover a wide spectrum. This section focuses on working directly with students in the media center. Even though teachers are encouraged to participate, what is emphasized here is your interaction with individual students, small groups, and entire classes. This activity culminates in a school-wide book fair. Forms are provided to accurately record services and programs that are normally hard to document.

BULLETIN BOARD RECORD (FORM 5-1)

Creating bulletin boards is a time-consuming chore, and good ones should be repeated after a few years. Even those that have not been your favorites may later spark a more imaginative display. To keep track of your ideas and efforts, maintain a file accompanied by a photograph of each display (Form 5-1). For durability the form may be posted onto a 3" × 5" card.

You can take either a slide, which should be put in a glassine envelope and taped to the front of the form, or a photograph, which should be mounted on the back of the form. If any special materials are needed to construct the board, be sure to note them.

RECORD OF BIBLIOGRAPHIES ON FILE (FORM 5-2)

You have many bibliographies on varying subjects and of varying lengths. Maintain a record of your file contents to help you stay aware of when they were last updated or acquired (Form 5-2). This will remind you to keep all bibliographies as current as your time and resources allow.

REFERENCE QUESTION FILE CARD (FORM 5-3)

A file of reference questions can serve many purposes. It can indicate areas in which the collection is weak if many questions on that subject go unanswered. It documents one of the services offered by the media center, and it alerts you to annual assignments by teachers.

To use Form 5-3, any staff member can enter the date, the question, the name of the individual who asked it, and the reason for which it was asked. You are the one to assign the subjects based on *Sears* or whatever seems most appropriate. Having the answer or knowing where it is located is extremely helpful when questions are repeated. Answers can be found by you or a staff member. Use the back of the form if more space is required. If a student has asked the question for a class assignment, include the teacher's name and grade level.

It is good practice to review the file regularly to weed out irrelevant questions from the past.

VIDEO-TAPING RECORDS (FORMS 5-4—5-6)

Preparing a video-tape program is time-consuming, but it frequently falls within the responsibility of the media specialist. You can quickly document the time taken by professionals, volunteers, and students to prepare a video-tape program by using Form 5-4. Longitudinal studies will indicate whether you are able to shorten the time involved.

For your permanent files, complete Form 5-5. It can be attached to the time study to give a comprehensive record of everything that went into the program.

An alternative record could be kept in a standard 3″ × 5″ format, using Form 5-6 as a guide, or as a reproducible form. It can be included as part of your regular shelf list or in a desk-top file box.

FORMS FOR WORKING WITH CLASSES (FORMS 5-7—5-14)

During the course of the school year, you will instruct many classes on different levels and subject areas. You teach some of these classes annually on a regular basis while others are taught on demand to meet a specific need.

In junior and senior high schools, teachers may wish to schedule their classes into the media center for one or more periods for instruction, research, or their own special use. Form 5-7 allows you to keep track of teacher reservations and to notify them by tearing off the bottom of the form when their classes are scheduled.

Very often these classes come to the media center to begin a research assignment. The teacher may request that you set aside a reserve collection for student use. With Form 5-8 you can be sure you know the scope of the teacher's plans and have a full range of material available. Special directions include a request to have publications only after a given copyright date, no overnight privileges on certain books, and the possible handling of a teacher's personal collection. Make a carbon copy of this form so the teacher will know exactly how much material has been placed on reserve. Have your clerk or volunteer type an itemized list including call numbers of the reserve collection, attach it to your copy of the request and file it for future use.

Use Form 5-9 to record skills taught to a specific grade or department throughout the year. For example, as shown on the sample here, if you teach third grades the meaning of fiction and nonfiction as well as the shelf arrangement, list "Fiction shelf arrangement," "Nonfiction shelf arrangement" under "Skill." Use the remaining columns to fill in the names of the third-grade teachers. When you have taught the skill to a specific class, enter the date under the teacher's name. In this way you see instantly what skills have been covered at a grade level as well as which classes are behind because of vacation or schedule changes.

If you keep monthly records for your own use or for administrative reports, Form 5-10 is a variation that might be more convenient. The left-hand

Library Media Skills Instruction				
Grade/Subject 3RD		School Year 81-82		
SKILL	FINCH	GAYDOS	VERDONI	KARMIN
Difference between fiction & non-fiction	10/27	10/28	10/28	10/23
Fiction shelf arrangement	11/10	11/11	11/11	11/19
Non-fiction shelf arrangement	11/17	11/18	11/18	12/3
100's	11/24	11/25	11/25	12/10
200's	12/8	12/9	12/9	12/17

FORM 5-9   Sample Library Media Skills Instruction Record

block is for grade/subject; then the next column is for the skill taught within that level. This is followed by a listing of teachers, not dates, because it is assumed the instruction was given some time during that month.

If you design games or library centers to be used in the classroom to reinforce skills, use Form 5-11 to keep track of who has them, what the parts used are, and the skill it reinforces.

Whether you teach bibliography as part of library skills or the classroom teacher teaches it, a guide to acceptable form should be available for teachers and/or students. Form 5-12 is suitable for students in grades 5 through 12.

Throughout the year you will read many stories. Use Form 5-13 for recording those read to a particular class. A story success rating of 1 to 5 can be assigned by you for future reference, 1 being the top and 5 being a story that did not work at all. You or the teacher may draw on this file for explanations of plot or styles of illustration that the entire class has experienced. You will also avoid accidentally repeating a story.

A cross-reference file (Form 5-14) can be kept on 3″ × 5″ cards so you can be sure that all students on the same grade level hear certain key stories. By using this file, you can see at a glance which classes have already heard the story without having to flip through the individual class sheets. Also in future years you can quickly tell if a group of second graders, for example, already heard a particular story when they were in first grade.

The clerical work can be done by a volunteer using Form 5-13 to record the information on Form 5-14. A check mark can be placed next to the date on the sheet to indicate that the information had been entered onto the 3″ × 5″ form.

CERTIFICATES AND AWARDS (FORMS 5-15, 5-16)

There are numerous occasions when you will wish to recognize outstanding performances, be it for mastery of skills, services rendered, or the winning of library contests.

Many of the supply houses for teachers and libraries sell printed certificates. (See the directory of such supply houses in the Appendix, page 247.) If your funds are limited, use Forms 5-15 and 5-16. The form with the owl (5-16) is more suitable for younger children.

If someone in your school is skilled in calligraphy or is particularly talented in drawing, persuade him or her to personalize one of these forms to include your school's name.

BOOK FAIR FORMS

An annual and much-anticipated occurrence in many media centers is a book fair. Whether you are officially responsible or whether it is a PTA/PTO program, your professional expertise is always welcome. By using these forms to facilitate proper organization, this complex operation can be run smoothly, thus reducing the disappointments that children experience when there are delays and incorrectly ordered books.

ANNOUNCEMENTS (FORMS 5-17, 5-18)

Handmade posters with the Book Fair date inserted at the bottom, such as that shown in Form 5-17, can be used to announce the forthcoming event, or you can use posters sent by the company that provides the books. Further announcements are made directly to the classes. Form 5-18, a sample of which is shown here, notifies the teachers of the upcoming fair.

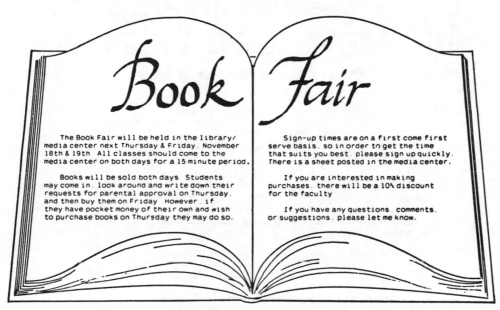

FORM 5-18   Sample Book Fair Notification to Teachers

SCHEDULING FORMS (FORMS 5-19, 5-20)

For elementary schools, classes will have to be scheduled twice—once for looking and once for buying the books. The sample scheduling form (Form 5-19) shows how that can be done. Notice that there are time slots for students who were absent or out of the classroom receiving special instruction when their class attended the fair. Secondary schools will use a more simple schedule since older students will need to make only one visit.

A last-minute reminder to the teacher (Form 5-20) is a good idea. Despite all signs and announcements, teachers occasionally forget. This reminder will avoid a scramble to contact the teacher when the class is late. Notification to parents of the book fair schedule is given in Section 8.

Book Fair Schedule					
TIME	MONDAY	TUESDAY	WEDNESDAY	THURSDAY	FRIDAY
9⁰⁵	Zinze / Ruby	Monday Absentees	Zinze / Ruby	Absentees	Absentees
9²⁵	Worles	A. m. Kindergarten	Worles	A. m. Kindergarten	Weck
10⁰⁵	Zahn / Lappin		Zahn / Lappin		Tenny
10²⁵	Compton	Sutter	Compton	Sutter	Bulla
11⁰⁵	Margolies	Walulak	Margolies	Walulak	Ruff
11²⁵	Rizzi	Tenny	Rizzi		Kaufman
12⁰⁵	Lunch	Lunch	Lunch	Lunch	Lunch
12²⁵	Sabados	Bierman	Sabados	Bierman	
1⁰⁵	O'Kelly	Nakielny	Beaubian	Nakielny	Call in order
1²⁵	Beaubian	P. m. Kindergarten	O'Kelly	P. m. Kindergarten	
2⁰⁵	Kaufman		Bulla		Complete Count of Money
2²⁵	Clean - up	Weck	Absentees	Ruff	Pack Up

FORM 5-19   Sample Book Fair Schedule

Southern Blvd. Media Center
BOOK FAIR

Your class is scheduled to come to the
media center on

Thursday at _____

and on Friday at _____

· · · ·   · · · ·   · · · ·   · · · ·

Would you please mention the following things to your class before you
come:

1. Students should look around and write down their requests on Thursday;
   they can then bring in the money to purchase the books on Friday. We will
   also sell books on Thursday if any students want to buy them that day.

2. Since 19 classes must have a turn in the media center each of the two
   days, it would be helpful if everyone comes in promptly, looks around,
   and makes a note of the books he or she wishes to buy and leaves.

3. For Thursday and Friday only, entrance to the media center will be
   through the regular door, but everyone will exit through the door at the
   back.

4. Please pass out the attached book request slips to your students ahead
   of time so that each one can write down his name and class before coming
   into the media center.

5. Each student should bring his own pencil with him when he comes.

6. Please ask them to try to have the correct amount of money so that we
   won't have too many large bills for which to make change.

Ruth Toor

FORM 5-20   Sample Book Fair Last-Minute Reminder

REQUEST FOR PURCHASE (FORM 5-21)

Elementary students may need parental approval for their selections. You can use the supplier's form, one of your own design, or the form provided at the end of this section (Form 5-21). If you make your own, include lines large enough and long enough to permit the young writer sufficient room to list titles. Even if you use the commercial form for the upper grades, you may still choose an in-house design for the lower grades so that adults do not have to write out the titles for young children.

SALES SLIPS AND ORDER CARDS (FORMS 5-22, 5-23)

Purchases should be recorded in duplicate. Cut a number of pieces of carbon paper to the proper size to make the writing simpler. Use the company's sales slips or use the one provided here (Form 5-22). To record books that need to be ordered, simply circle the title on the sales slip, making sure it is exactly correct.

Later the books to be ordered can be transferred to 3″ × 5″ cards (Form 5-23) to make telephoning the order easy. The card should include the title, author, price, and tally marks, as shown on the sample here. When the books arrive they can be matched with the sales slips for delivery.

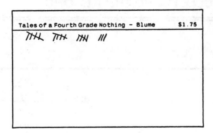

FORM 5-23   Sample Book Fair Order Card

MONEY COLLECTION FORM (FORM 5-24)

In your book fair file, keep a culminating statement showing the amount of money collected, profit made, and the date of the payment made to the company (Form 5-24). This is useful for comparison purposes and may be the basis for changing companies or continuing with the same company.

BULLETIN BOARD RECORD

Title _____

Month _____ Year _____

Special Needs:

_____

_____

_____

SLIDE

BULLETIN BOARD RECORD

Title _____

Month _____ Year _____

Special Needs:

_____

_____

_____

SLIDE

FORM 5-1   Bulletin Board Record

Record of Bibliographies on File

Subject	Number of Items	Updated

FORM 5-2   Record of Bibliographies on File

```
┌─────────────────────────────────────────────┬───────────┐
│                                             │  DATE     │
│  SUBJECT(S): _____  │           │
│                                             │           │
│  _____  │           │
├─────────────────────────────────────────────┴───────────┤
│  QUESTION: _____  │
├──────────────────────────────────────────────────────────┤
│  ANSWER/LOCATION: _____  │
│                                                          │
│  _____  │
├──────────────────────────────────────────────────────────┤
│  REQUESTED BY: _____  │
│  PURPOSE: _____  │
│                                                          │
└──────────────────────────────────────────────────────────┘
```

FORM 5-3   Reference Question File Card

Video Taping Time Study

	PAID STAFF state title	TIME Hours	Min.	STUDENTS or VOLUNTEERS	TIME Hours	Min.
ORGANIZATION						
1. Writing audio script						
2. Writing video script						
3. Reviewing script for continuity						
Total Time						
PREPARATION						
1. Assembling components—including blank tape						
2. Cleaning equipment						
3. Moving equipment to shooting location						
4. Setting up equipment						
Total Time						
TAPING						
1. "Dress Rehearsal"—includes time of technical crew, talent, supervising teachers, etc.						
2. Show—includes time of technical crew, talent, supervising teachers, etc.						
Total Time						
POST-TAPING						
1. Playing back tape to check quality						
2. Disassembling equipment						
3. Returning equipment to storage						
4. Screening production—equals total preparation time, show time, disassembling and returning equipment						
GRAND TOTAL TIME						

FORM 5-4   Video Taping Time Study

Video Tape Program Record

Call number _____ Date _____

_____

Title _____

_____

Class _____

Teacher _____

Students on Camera _____

_____

_____

_____

_____

_____

_____

_____

_____

Students off Camera (makeup, director, etc.) _____

_____

_____

_____

_____

_____

_____

_____

_____

FORM 5-5   Video Tape Program Record

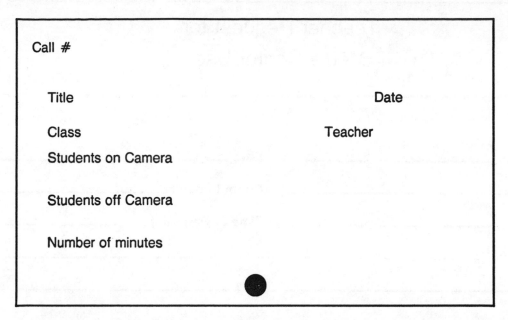

Call #

Title   Date

Class   Teacher

Students on Camera

Students off Camera

Number of minutes

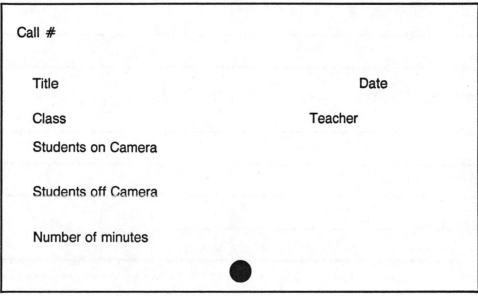

Call #

Title   Date

Class   Teacher

Students on Camera

Students off Camera

Number of minutes

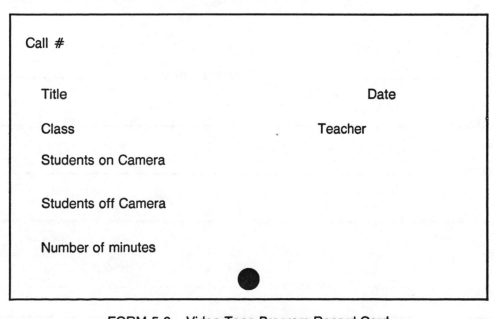

Call #

Title   Date

Class   Teacher

Students on Camera

Students off Camera

Number of minutes

FORM 5-6   Video Tape Program Record Card

Teacher Request for
Media Center Use

Teacher _____   Date _____

Subject/Grade _____   Room Number _____

Day and Date _____   Time or Period(s) _____

Reason for Request _____

_____

_____

_____

_____

Is instruction necessary?   ☐ Yes   ☐ No

Area of instruction _____

_____

_____

Number of students in class _____

· ·

To _____   Room Number _____

Day and Date Scheduled _____

Time or Period(s) Scheduled _____

Signed _____

Request for Reserve Collection

Teacher _____ Date _____

Subject/Grade _____ Room Number _____

Topic _____

_____

Reserved material to include:

☐ Books   ☐ Periodicals   ☐ Vertical File

          ☐ Microforms   ☐ Nonprint Material

Materials are to be on reserve

from _____ to _____

Special Directions _____

_____

_____

_____

_____

Amount of material reserved:

Books _____ Periodicals _____ Vertical File _____

Microforms _____ Nonprint Material _____

Comments _____

_____

Signed _____ **Date** _____

FORM 5-8   Request for Reserve Collection

Library Media Skills Instruction

Grade/Subject _____   School Year _____

SKILL				

FORM 5-9   Library Media Skills Instruction Record

Library Skills Combined Report

Month _____   Year _____

Grade/Subject	Skill Taught	Teacher	Teacher	Teacher	Teacher

FORM 5-10   Library Skills Combined Report

Library Media Skills
Instructional Materials Record

Skill Reinforced _____

No. of Copies/Sets

Components _____

Teacher	Date Out	Date In

FORM 5-11   Library Media Skills Instructional Materials Record

BIBLIOGRAPHIC FORM

1. For a book:

   Author. <u>Title</u>. City of publication: Publisher, Copyright, Number of Pages.

   Example:
   Sperry, Armstrong. <u>All about the Arctic and the Antarctic</u>. New York: Random House, 1957, 146 p.

   For a book with two authors:

   Author (last name, first name) and second author (first name, last name). <u>Title</u>. City of publication: Publisher, Copyright, Number of Pages

   Example:
   Murphy, Barbara Beasley and Norman Baker. <u>Thor Heyerdahl and the Reed Boat Ra</u>. New York: Lippincott, 1974, 64 p.

2. For an encyclopedia article:

   "Article," <u>Encyclopedia Name</u>. Volume number, Last copyright, Pages.

   Example:
   "Ethiopia," <u>The New Book of Knowledge</u>. V. 5, 1978, pp. 296-301.

3. For a magazine article:

   Author (if known). "Article," <u>Magazine</u>. Date, Page.

   Example:
   Cumming, Joseph E., Jr. "Terrible Twists of Fate," <u>National Wildlife</u>. June/July 1980, p. 29.

4. For a filmstrip:

   "Title of Strip," <u>Title of Series</u> (Filmstrip). Producer, Copyright (if available).

   Example:
   "Keeping Well," <u>Good Health Habits</u> (Filmstrip). Coronet Instructional Media, 1968.

5. For a study print:

   "Title of Print," <u>Name of Series</u> (Study Print). Producer, Copyright.

   Example:
   "Rain," <u>Weather Phenomena</u> (Study Print). Instructional Aids, 1968.

FORM 5-12   Bibliographic Form Sheet for Students

Storytelling Record

Teacher _____   **Grade** _____

Date	Author	Title	Rating

FORM 5-13   Storytelling Record Form

Storytelling Record Card

Author _____

Title _____

Class	Date	Class	Date

Storytelling Record Card

Author _____

Title _____

Class	Date	Class	Date

Storytelling Record Card

Author _____

Title _____

Class	Date	Class	Date

FORM 5-14   Storytelling Record Card

An Award
for

_____

is made to _____

_____   _____
Date   Signed

FORM 5-15   Library Service Award

An Award for

_____

*is made to*_____

_____   _____
Date   *Signed*

FORM 5-16   Library Service Award for Young Children

FORM 5-17 Book Fair Announcement

FORM 5-18   Book Fair Notification Format

Book Fair Schedule

TIME	MONDAY	TUESDAY	WEDNESDAY	THURSDAY	FRIDAY

FORM 5-19   Book Fair Schedule

BOOKS I WOULD LIKE

Title	Price

Name: _____   Room Number: _____

FORM 5-21   Book Purchase Request Form

SALES SLIP

NAME _____   CLASS _____

PRICE   TITLE

FORM 5-22   Sales Slip

BOOK FAIR—MONEY COLLECTION

Book Fair Dates _____

Total Checks $ _____

Total Wrapped Coins $ _____

Total Loose Coins $ _____

Total Collected $ _____

                    — Profit $ _____

Total Sent to Company $ _____

Date Sent _____

FORM 5-24   Book Fair Money Collection Form

Section 6

Forms for Working with Teachers

I WONDER IF ROLLER SKATES WOULD BE BETTER?

Communicating with teachers is one of your regular tasks, and you must usually initiate the contact. It is important that teachers realize how much you can help them.

You must constantly interrelate with teachers to effectively develop joint programs and to enhance students' skills. The forms in this chapter record the two-way communication process that must exist to fully utilize media resources. Familiarizing teachers with available services includes making schedules, notices, and requests; employing classroom aids; and receiving feedback from teachers.

ORIENTATION FORMS (FORMS 6-1—6-3)

Teachers new to your building need to be given an orientation to the media center. Even if they have had experience in other schools, practices differ and misunderstandings can be prevented by making sure everyone understands your procedures. Try to arrange the orientation session quickly. (It would be ideal if the orientation could be conducted before classes begin, but this is not always possible.) Form 6-1 provides a sign-up schedule for teachers. Only a half hour is allotted per session. Once you discover the needs of individual teachers, further sessions can be scheduled if necessary. To fix the schedule, bring this form to each of the new teachers. These visits will give you an opportunity to follow up the contacts you made earlier, as noted in Section 2.

As part of this orientation session, use Form 6-2, the Hardware Training Checklist. Three columns have been left untitled so that you can write in the names of the special equipment you own for which training is necessary. The columns below the titles allow you to include more than a simple check mark. If you own more than one brand or model of 16mm projector, for example, it is not necessary to show each teacher how to run each model. Just record the type of equipment you demonstrated.

Students also need to be given an orientation to the media center. If you have a faculty meeting before the students arrive, show the teachers Form 6-3 (a class sign-up orientation schedule) with time slots included. If the teachers cannot fill it out immediately, tell them that you will bring it to them within the next few days.

The lowest grade in the school should be given the highest priority for an early orientation. After their needs are met, you can decide how much time to allot to the upper grades.

PRACTICE BOOK CARDS (FORM 6-4)

Elementary schools have a special problem: the children in the lowest grade, whether it is kindergarten or first grade, are not only new to the building, they are new to school itself. Any help you can give to familiarize them with the procedures of the media center will smooth their transition to school.

Use Form 6-4, Practice Book Cards, to acquaint them with the size of the book cards, the size of the line used, and the general format. When you run off copies of the cards, be sure they are an exact facsimile of the cards you use. Each student is given one card to practice writing his or her name and to learn the room number or classroom code to be placed in the right-hand column.

SCHEDULES (FORMS 6-5, 6-6)

Your media center will generally operate under one of two schedules. You will be either fully scheduled (part of a teacher's preparation time) or open. If you are fully scheduled, you have little flexibility. If you have an open schedule, you can try to arrange your week to meet both your needs and those of the teachers.

In an elementary school you must balance giving instruction with storytelling. Giving instruction need not be continuous at a grade level, but can evolve in blocks throughout the year to fulfill curriculum requirements. Weekly scheduled lessons are not the only, nor necessarily the best, approach to teaching skills. You might present such a unit in five sessions on five consecutive days. Storytelling should be an ongoing activity, but you must decide how many grade levels to include.

These two schedules (full or open) are not the only ones available. Students may not have free access to a media center staffed by a part-time library media specialist. In such a situation, you must be even more creative and flexible in designing your schedule. Form 6-5 is a sample schedule for a library media specialist who is present for only half a day. Teachers block in the times to bring in their classes when the library is not being covered. The

		Library Media Specialist's Schedule			
TIME	MONDAY	TUESDAY	WEDNESDAY	THURSDAY	FRIDAY
9:15 - 9:45	Karmin Library	Finch Library	Yudoni Library		N.I. + N.I.2 Stories
9:45 - 10:15	Skills	Skills	Skills	2nd Grade Stories	
10:15 - 10:45					E.D. Stories
10:45 - 11:15				Kindergarten Stories	
11:15 - 11:45	1st Grade Stories		3rd Grade Stories		
11:45 - 12:15		4th Grade Stories		P.I.1 + P.I.2 Stories	5th Grade Stories
12:15 - 12:45		Teachers' self-schedule below			Keenan/Holland
12:45 - 1:15	Strambach		Feroch/Bitting	Hyman	
1:15 - 1:45		Romanczyk			Dietsch
1:45 - 2:15	5th Grade	Samuels	4th Grade		Gaydos
2:15 - 2:45	Classes	Pastrick	Classes	Tice/Marcello	O'Connor

AM - open schedule (Library media specialist present)
PM - fixed Schedule

FORM 6-5   Sample Library Media Specialist's Schedule

schedule is more open when the library media specialist is present; then students can do research or borrow materials during any open time in the morning. A blank Form 6-5 is provided at the end of this section for individualizing the schedule.

If you belong to a cooperative 16mm film library and if films are routed through the media center, you must have a method of notifying teachers of what is coming in. Form 6-6 shows a sample week's schedule. The numbers assigned to each film can be used by the teachers when they sign up (see Form 3-20). The teacher who ordered the film has first priority in showing it, but anyone else may also use it.

SOUTHERN BOULEVARD MEDIA CENTER

Film Delivery for the Week of 10/21/82 to 10/28/82

	Title	Teacher
1.	Paper Money	Lanning
2.	Family Life in Japan	Lanning
3.	Kite Story	Lanning
4.	Circulation and Human Body	Sexton
5.	Mechanisms of Breathing	Sexton
6.	Colonial Expansion	Paddock
7.	French Explorers	Paddock
8.	Flight of Apollo 15	Boone
9.	Father of the Space Age	Boone

FORM 6-6   Sample Film Schedule

SPECIAL NOTICES (FORMS 6-7—6-11)

To keep teachers aware of the new materials that have been added to the media center collection, take the time to send them a brief annotated bibliography now and then. Form 6-7 is an example of such a notice. Many teachers

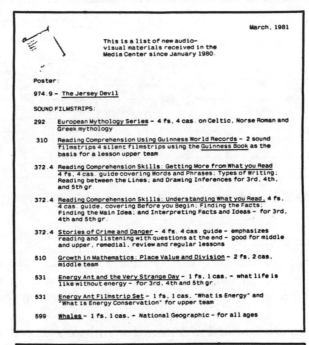

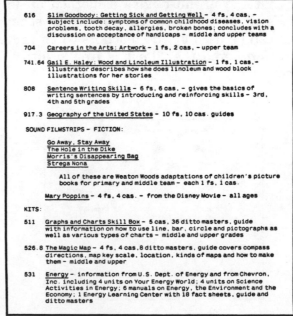

FORM 6-7   Sample Bibliography Sheet of New Materials

file these bibliographies and use them as a basis for making later requests. By informing the teachers, you are stimulating the circulation of new materials.

Publicize the media center within your school by sending short announcements of interesting happenings to teachers. Form 6-8 is a sample announcement. If you send them out regularly, a clerk or volunteer can easily handle the task. As more teachers use the media center to display their class projects and the number of events in the media center increases, so will the traffic.

To encourage greater circulation of professional periodicals, try using Form 6-9 instead of the usual routing sheet. Make a ditto listing titles of journals to which you subscribe. Next to each title, write or type in the date of the issue and below the title describe one or two articles of general interest. Post this form both in the teachers' room and on central office bulletin boards. A sample sheet is shown here. This method, while not foolproof, may alert teachers to topics relevant to their activities.

If you have a vertical file containing pictures, pamphlets, and clippings, let your teachers know what subjects it contains. Form 6-10 is a sample listing of subjects. When teachers give students assignments, they will find such a listing helpful in reminding students to broaden the scope of their research beyond books and encyclopedias.

If you have produced special materials, such as transparencies of maps, for students to enlarge to poster size, or slide shows of local ecology, or perhaps even library skills units designed for classroom centers, use Form 6-11 to alert teachers to their availability. You might then receive requests and suggestions for future projects.

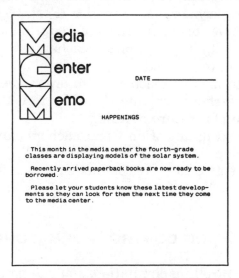

FORM 6-8   Sample Media Center "Happenings" Sheet

ARTICLES OF INTEREST

ARITHMETIC TEACHER _____ May, 1981 _____

p. 19 "Ideas"

Four excellent ideas about how to teach computer
programming without a computer. In addition to
familiarizing students with how computers work, the
ideas help to develop logical, analytical thinking.

p. 26 "Fractions: Results and Implications from
National Assessment"

Results obtained after testing 9- and 13-year olds
indicate that students have only a rote procedure
for adding fractions, that they have difficulty in
understanding fractions on a number line, and that
they experience other problems. Teaching
implications are considered.

INSTRUCTOR _____ May, 1981 _____

p. 72 "How to Get Your Project Funded"

A brief step-by-step plan on how to find the right
foundation, how to write the proposal, and what to
do when you hear from the foundation.

LEARNING _____ April/May, 1981 _____

p. 102 "Baseball: A Big Hit at Year's End"

With six more weeks of school left, a bright idea for
a bulletin board took off and motivated learning in
all areas of the curriculum- - - and the teacher knew
nothing about the subject!!

FORM 6-9   Sample Periodical Articles of Interest Sheet

TEACHER INPUT FORMS (FORMS 6-12, 6-13)

Involve teachers in the ordering process in two ways. First, have them suggest books, periodicals, and other materials they would like to have added to the collection. Send each teacher a notice (Form 6-12) requesting suggestions—either specific titles or descriptions of materials needed in general subject areas. Responses will improve once teachers see that their colleagues receive materials they have ordered.

The second way to involve teachers is to order audio-visual materials on preview and to have teachers evaluate them. Form 6-13 allows you to record their opinions and yours for future ordering.

Another valuable communication from teachers can be obtained by using the Teacher Evaluation of Library Media Program, Form 9-22. When teachers know that you are receptive to their comments, they will become increasingly willing to make them.

CIRCULATION CONTROL FORM (FORM 6-14)

As an expert in controlling circulation, you can assist teachers in keeping track of their own classroom collections. Teachers frequently have auxiliary sets of books that they allow students to borrow overnight. Since there are no

```
                    SOUTHERN BOULEVARD MEDIA CENTER

                    VERTICAL FILE          September, 1982

                         Subject Headings

    Africa                          Industries
    Agriculture                     Insects
    Alaska                          Inventors
    Amphibians                      Islands
    Animals (General)
    Antarctica                      Japan
    Archeology & Fossils
      (Dinosaurs)                   Law
    Architecture                    Libraries & Books
    Arizona                         Light & Electricity
    Arts & Artists
    Asia                            Mammals (Land & Water)
    Astronomy                       Maps (U.S., Foreign)
    Australia—New Guinea            Mathematics
    Authors (A-M, N-Z,              Metric System
      General)                      Mexico
    Automobiles                     Middle East
                                    Moon (See also Space)
    Bermuda Triangle                Money
    Birds                           Monsters (Bigfoot)
  * Black History                   Morris County
                                    Mountains
    Canada                          Music
    Careers & Occupations           Mythology
  * Caves
    Chatham Township                National Parks
    China                           New Jersey
    Communications                * New York City
    Communities
    Conservation (Wildlife)         Ocean Life
  * Consumer Information
    Costumes                        Personalities in U.S. History
    Cowboys                         Pets
    Crafts                          Plants
                                    Pollution
    Deserts                         Pond & Marsh Life
    Diseases                        Presidents—U.S.
    Dolls                           Puerto Rico
    Drugs
                                    Recreation & Games (See also
    Earthquakes                       Sports)
    Ecology (See also               Reptiles
      Pollution)                    Rocks
    Economics
    Egypt                           Safety
    Energy                          Science
    Europe (A-F, G-Z)               Seasons (Scenery)
    Explorers                       Soil
                                    Solar System
    Fire Prevention                 South America
    Fish (See also Ocean            Space
      Life)                         Sports (See also Recreation)
    Flags
    Flowers                         Teacher Resources
    Food (See also Health &         Tools
      Nutrition)                    Transportation
    Fuel (Coal, Gas, Oil—See        Trees
      also Energy)
                                    United Nations
    Geography                       United States (A-L, M-Z)
    Great Britain                   United States History
                                    United States Politics &
    Hawaii                            Government
    Health and Nutrition (See also
      Food)                         Volcanoes
    Holidays and Holiday Customs
    Horses                          Wars
    Human Body                      Washington, D.C.
                                    Water
    Iceland                         Weather
  * Immigrants                    * Women
    India                           World Leaders
    Indians                         Writing, Creative

        * Denotes files in special need of additional materials.
```

FORM 6-10   Sample Vertical File

library cards or pockets in these books, to maintain circulation control you may suggest the use of Form 6-14, which uses copy numbers that are to be placed inside each book. This form can also be used for interdepartmental loans within the school. For example, the reading department may offer a series of books to a classroom teacher by adapting this form.

NOTICE FROM THE MEDIA CENTER

Orientations for teachers new to this building will be given at the times and dates listed below. Please sign up for the times most convenient for you. Anyone wishing a "refresher" course on operating equipment may feel free to sign up as well.

September ____

_____ AM   _____ PM

September ____

_____ AM   _____ PM

September ____

_____ AM   _____ PM

September ____

_____ AM   _____ PM

FORM 6-1   Teacher Orientation Sign-up Sheet

Date _____

Hardware Training Checklist

Teacher	16mm Projector	Filmstrip Projector	Cassette Recorder	Overhead Projector	Slide Projector			

PLEASE SIGN UP TO BRING YOUR CLASS TO THE MEDIA CENTER FOR ORIENTATION

WEEK OF _____

TIME	MONDAY	TUESDAY	WEDNESDAY	THURSDAY	FRIDAY

FORM 6-3   Class Orientation Sign-up Sheet

| FIC | | 19.432 |
| GAN | | |

Gantos, Jack
Sleepy Ronald

Date Due	Borrower's Name	

| 629.4 | | 16.917 |
| COL | | |

Colby, Carroll
Moon exploration

Date Due	Borrower's Name	

| FIC | | 19.432 |
| GAN | | |

Gantos, Jack
Sleepy Ronald

Date Due	Borrower's Name	

| 629.4 | | 16.917 |
| COL | | |

Colby, Carroll
Moon exploration

Date Due	Borrower's Name	

FORM 6-4   Practice Book Cards

Library Media Specialist's Schedule

TIME	MONDAY	TUESDAY	WEDNESDAY	THURSDAY	FRIDAY

FORM 6-5   Library Media Specialist's Schedule

Media Center Memo

Date _____

PLEASE FILE FOR FUTURE REFERENCE

The following materials have been made by teachers
or students and are available for classroom use.

Type of Material	Prepared by Date	Title/Components

FORM 6-11   Record of Library-Produced Materials

Media Center Memo

SEND US YOUR REQUESTS

Do you have any recommendations for books, periodicals, or software that should be added to the media center collection?

Fill in the appropriate information as well as you can. We will be glad to order them.

Author (If applicable)	Title	Publisher/ Producer	Price

FROM _____   DATE _____

FORM 6-12   Teacher Request for Purchase

MEDIA EVALUATION

Title:

FORMAT: Book style ☐ Box style ☐

DIMENSIONS:

KIT ☐   **FILMSTRIP** ☐   **OTHER** _____

CONTENTS:

PRODUCER:

ADDRESS:

ORGANIZATION OF TEACHER'S GUIDE

Overall rating _____ Number of pages _____

Positive features: _____

CATALOG NUMBER: **PRICE:**

SUBJECT AREA(S): _____

Negative features: _____

LIBRARY MEDIA SPECIALIST EVALUATION

COMMENTS: _____

TEACHER EVALUATION

	POOR	FAIR	GOOD	EXCELLENT
Relation to curriculum	☐	☐	☐	☐
Organization of contents	☐	☐	☐	☐
Material on student level	☐	☐	☐	☐
Clarity of purpose	☐	☐	☐	☐
Technical quality of visuals	☐	☐	☐	☐
Technical quality of sound	☐	☐	☐	☐
Usefulness of manual	☐	☐	☐	☐
Quality of supp. materials	☐	☐	☐	☐

COMMENTS: _____

RECOMMENDATION:

We Need This! _____

It Would Help _____

Forget it! _____

Teacher's Signature   Date

Returned to Producer _____ Ordered _____ Purchase Order No. _____
           Date   Date

Reviewed in _____ Date/Page _____

FORM 6-13   Teacher Preview Evaluation Form

CIRCULATION CONTROL

DEPARTMENT _____

TITLE _____

PUBLISHER _____   NO. COPIES _____

COPY NO.	DATE OUT	BORROWER	DATE RET'D

　　　　FORM 6-14　Circulation Control Form

Section 7

WHEN I WAS
HIRED THEY TOLD
ME I WAS EXPECTED
TO KEEP ON THE BALL.

Forms for Working with the Administration

$\mathbf{T}$he administration controls the environment in which you work. It establishes the limits of your decision-making, the methods you may use for selection and purchase, and the funds you have available. To operate efficiently, you must know and have a record of these boundaries and how you comply with them. Forms in this section include your record of district policies and samples of your reports and requests to the administration.

RECORDS OF DISTRICT POLICIES (FORMS 7-1, 7-2)

You become so accustomed to the forms needed to manage your media center that you often overlook the special ones required to communicate with the administration. For someone new to a district, the local practices are frequently confusing and invariably different from those encountered previously. Instead of repeatedly asking the same questions, use Form 7-1 to quickly learn what policies and regulations directly affect you and how you are expected to keep the administration aware of your activities. Even an established library media specialist can forget just how many copies of a report or request are to be submitted. Form 7-1 is your at-hand source. Use the blank lines to make any additions relevant to your district.

Classroom Repair List

Form 7-2, a Classroom Repair List, noted on Form 7-1 as "Repair Requests" is an example of what you need to have on file. It is your responsibility to observe and report any repairs such as broken light fixtures, faulty switches, peeling paint, or nonfunctioning heating units in the media center. Depending on the district, this form can be used both throughout the year and as a final roundup.

Forms for Acquisition of Materials

Every district has its own forms for purchasing. Obviously you must use these. Learn what they are as quickly as possible. You need to know the difference between items put out for bid and those that can be ordered directly from your chosen vendor. There may be a different form for each. Does your district allow you to take advantage of special price offers by accepting delivery of materials to be followed by a confirming purchase order? If you are permitted to do so, you can often save a considerable amount of money at conventions and other meetings. However, don't assume that your district permits this practice without checking in advance.

Budget requests are the first step in acquisition and again you use your district's form to submit your recommendations. Many states now require very specific descriptions of each budget item. To make certain you receive what you truly want, give as much information as possible. This saves time by eliminating the need to refer to the original catalog later, and increases the likelihood that you will be satisfied when the item is delivered.

FORMS LEADING TO REPORTS (FORMS 7-3—7-5)

Before you file a report on activities such as a professional meeting or workshop, or just an account of what is happening in the media center, you may need to complete a preliminary form. Form 7-3 is a sample request for a professional day. (For the written report on this workshop, see Form 7-6.) It is a good idea to be as specific as possible when describing the purpose of your attendance. Often, a copy of this form is filed with your permanent record folder.

The Monthly Planning Guide (Form 7-4), in combination with the Daily Planning Guide (Form 7-5), will help simplify the preparation of your monthly report. The Monthly Planning Guide serves as a reminder of upcoming scheduled events and lets you judge your priorities for the month. You can note specific items ahead of time, such as a budget falling due or an upcoming project with a teacher. The filled-in samples of Forms 7-4 and 7-5 will give you ideas for using these forms in concert.

The Daily Planning Guide (Form 7-5) is structured to serve your needs and can replace the teacher's plan book that most library media specialists now use. It also provides the documentation necessary for accountability. Just list the activities you have scheduled with both classes and teachers under "Scheduled Events" as in the sample shown here. The left-hand column is for the time period. The right-hand column, "Prep Time," is your estimation of how long it will take you to prepare for this event. For example, if you are giving a book talk, you will need at least 30–45 minutes to choose your topic, select appropriate books from the shelves, and briefly review the contents. On the other hand, showing a filmstrip may require only five minutes to set it up in the projector and make sure it is focused and working correctly.

SAYREVILLE SCHOOL DISTRICT
PROFESSIONAL DAY REQUEST FORM

NAME _____ Hilda K. Weisburg _____

SCHOOL/OFFICE _____ Truman/Eisenhower _____

POSITION _____ Library Media Specialist _____

DATE OF REQUEST _____ April 4, 1981 _____

PROFESSIONAL DAY(S) REQUESTED _____ One _____

PURPOSE To attend an Institute at Trenton State College sponsored by
_____ the Educational Media Association of New Jersey. _____
_____ Of special interest is a series of workshops on the micro computer. _____

TOTAL EXPENSES REQUESTED: _____ 16.90 _____

Registration/Tuition _____ 5.00 _____

Mileage/Transportation _____ 11.90 (85 miles @ .14 per mile) _____

Meals _____ does not apply _____

Accommodations _____ does not apply _____

Other _____

SUBSTITUTE NEEDED _____ No _____
(If so, name.)

Hilda K. Weisburg
Signature

PRINCIPAL'S RECOMMENDATION _____ DATE _____

PROFESSIONAL DAYS TAKEN TO DATE _____ One _____

CC: Personnel File

FORM 7-3   Sample Professional Day Request

LIBRARY MEDIA SPECIALIST'S MONTHLY PLANNING GUIDE

Month _October_   Year _1982_

Classes
  5th Grade - Subject Encyclopedias Unit
  6th Grade - Book Talk
  Kindergarten - Orientation - EARLY

Clerical Tasks
  Filing catalog cards
  Typing budget requests
  Processing new books

Special Inservice on Overhead Projectors
  PTO meeting - Back-to-School Night
  Budget - final submission
  4th Grade - Unit on Earthquakes/Volcanoes

FORM 7-4   Sample Library Media Specialist's Monthly Planning Guide

	Library Media Specialist's Daily Planning Guide			Date: _Tuesday October 19, 1982_		
SCHEDULED EVENTS			**THINGS TO DO**			
Scheduled Time	Event	Prep Time	Priority	Description		Completed
10:15 – 10:45	_Story visit – 3rd grade_	_10 min. selection time_	_1_	_Set up for in-service – at 2:00 PM_		_20 min_
11:15 – 12:15	_5th grade unit – "subject encyclopedias" Objective: students will be able to use an index to locate information in a nonalphabetically arranged encyclopedia._	_3 hrs._	_1_	_Review material to be used with 5th graders_		_15 min._
	Assessment: Observation of students during actual research		_2_	_Have volunteer put out assortment of subject ency- clopedias on a table._		✓
1:45 – 2:15	_Kindergarten stories_	_10 min. selection time_	_3_	_Pull books for next week's book talk to 5th grade – "Diaries & Journals"_		_30 mins._
2:30 – 4:00	_In-service – using the overhead projector_	_4 hrs._	_3_	_Prepare classroom unit on "Earthquakes & Volcanoes" for next Tuesday delivery_		_35 mins._
			_2_	_Teach Mrs. B (volunteer) to check Bookfinder against card catalog_		_10 mins._
			Emergency	_Bulb on filmstrip proj. burned out – gave replace- ment & changed bulb_		✓ _15 mins_

FORM 7-5   Sample Library Media Specialist's Daily Planning Guide

If your supervisor requires formal written objectives and assessments for teaching units, there is room in the Scheduled Events section for you to record them. You might want to include objectives in any case for your own personal guidelines, but the decision is yours.

The "Things to Do" section will include not only your preparation for events scheduled for that day, but also two other types of activities: long-range planning and operational responsibilities. Long-range planning for complicated lessons such as a library scavenger hunt may entail five hours of preparation time spread over a two-week period. You can slot these five hours in small task sections over the next ten days, seeing how it will fit into your schedule. The second activity included in "Things to Do" is concerned with operational responsibilities such as cataloging time, preparing reports, maintaining a-v equipment, training staff, and so on. Each item should be described using an imperative verb such as "write, clean, explain." Assign priorities using either letters or numbers to focus your attention on the most important items first. Using such a form is considered a good time-management practice in industry. Such a technique can prove invaluable to help hard-pressed library media specialists cope with constant time pressures.

REPORTS (FORMS 7-6—7-11)

Districts generally require you to submit a report after you have attended a professional meeting. A sample is given in Form 7-6. When preparing this report, remember that a copy is often placed in your permanent record folder

TO:
From:
Subject: Professional Day

On Saturday, April 4, 1981, I attended an all-day institute at Trenton State College sponsored by the Educational Media Association of New Jersey. The three workshops I selected dealt with the micro or home computer.

WORKSHOP I 9:30-11:00—Introduction to the Microcomputer
    Presentation by Martin T. Skeele, Computer Analyst, Vydec, Inc.
This was an excellent introduction to computer terminology with emphasis on the microcomputer. I now understand thoroughly its three main components. The input is similar to a typewriter keyboard and the output is basically a television monitor. A printer can be attached as an additional output device. Computers are divided into three parts: the memory where data is stored, the arithmetic-logic unit which performs computations and logic functions, and the control unit which determines what operation is to be performed next. A simple program was demonstrated and then "translated" into seven of the most common programming languages. Various input/output devices and storage media were explained.

WORKSHOP II 11:00-12:15—Comparison of Microcomputers
    Presentation by Tom Tolley, Sales Representative, Stonehenge
    Computers, Summit, N.J.

A chart comparing the three leading microcomputers—Commodore PET, the APPLE, and the TRS80-III were shown. The specific advantages and disadvantages of each were discussed. The charts are attached for your information.

WORKSHOP III 2:15-3:15—Developing a Computer-Related Curriculum
    Presentation by Dr. Jerry Kaplan, Prof. of Math Education,
    Seton Hall University

Microcomputers have three main uses:
    CAI or Computer Assisted Instruction. This is the area most people
    think of when they consider computers. Although much software
    is available, the quality has been poor. The larger publishing
    houses are now getting involved in its production and quality
    may improve.

    Management Systems. Recordkeeping is the main area for computer
    use in the future. It is easy to keep track of the number of
    students in a math program and which tests they need to take. The
    tests themselves can be stored in the computer.

    Programming. From first grade on, students can be taught to
    program. Preparing students to be computer literate is a
    necessary part of today's education. The development of logical
    thinking is a great benefit of programming training.

CONCLUSION
The workshops provided the best overall view of microcomputers that I have had. An enormous amount of information was dispensed; my notes are extensive. The implications for this district are obvious: The computer is here to stay, the cost is not high, and the benefit to students is great.

FORM 7-6   Sample Professional Day Report

and will demonstrate your ability to communicate clearly. Try to be as brief as possible, preferably using one page or less. If you have additional information, refer to it and leave it to your administrator to request further details. Since so many papers are required reading for administrators, brevity is always appreciated.

An interim report can be sent whenever a problem surfaces or if something special is happening in the media center. Form 7-7 is an example. While the information could have been included in a monthly report, a separate note focuses your supervisor's attention on the problem and is more likely to produce an immediate response.

If your district requires a monthly report, you can get the job done more quickly by using an outline so that each month's narrative will have a similar structure. Form 7-8 can be used as a guide for developing your own working outline. Form 7-9 shows a sample report developed from such an outline. Again, it should be as brief as possible. If you plan to attach statistical records, Forms 3-36 through 3-40 can be used.

Even if your district does not require an annual report, it is a good idea to prepare one to document your activities for the year as well as to reassess

To:

From:

Subject: Science in a Shoebox

A parent volunteer has been checking our Science in a Shoebox experiments as they are returned by the children and restocking and resupplying them so they can recirculate. She comes in one hour a week to do this.

She and I both feel that, with the heavy use these boxes have been getting, our supplies are running out and some of the handmade materials that go into the boxes need to be refurbished and replaced. This is time consuming and requires an outlay of funds. It is really not fair to the children to circulate experiment boxes which are not in good repair.

Our problem is this: We need several additional volunteers and approximately $40. Perhaps the P.T.O. might be of some service. Do you have any other solution to ease our problem?

FORM 7-7   Sample Interim Report

MEDIA CENTER REPORT
January 1982

STATISTICS
  CIRCULATION
    STUDENTS

Nonfiction	1,986	
Fiction	1,856	
TOTAL	3,842	
STAFF		
Nonfiction	158	
Fiction	49	
TOTAL	207	
TOTAL CIRCULATION FOR JANUARY		4,049
AVERAGE DAILY STUDENT		
CIRCULATION		170
BOOKS ADDED TO THE COLLECTION		50
BOOKS DISCARDED		4
SKILLS CLASSES		8

Average daily circulation statistics for January show a slight drop from the high of the first months of the school year. This may be attributed to winter doldrums or a slow start on new assignments after the holidays. It should be noted, however, that over 4,000 books, more than half of the collection, circulated.

Although several volunteers did not show up during their regularly scheduled times because of post-holiday demands at home, we were able to catalog and process many of the paperbacks that arrived shortly before vacation.

A full-length book is being read with the third grade during their storytelling time. This activity promotes listening skills without the usual visual stimulation, develops an interest in good literature, and encourages students to read more difficult books.

Two of the volunteers are busy weeding the pamphlet file. Materials here are ephemeral in nature and not sturdy. We should complete the weeding by the end of April.

Both the picture file and the reference collection are experiencing heavier than normal use. Teachers in the lower grades are requiring more research from their students.

A major problem this month has been the down time of the 16mm projectors. The problem will be discussed with the vendor who handles our service contract to determine if it is caused by the age of the projectors or poor understanding of operating techniques by teachers, and a memo containing both vendor's recommendations and personal comments will be submitted. If it appears that incorrect operating techniques are causing the problem, some workshops will be scheduled before and after school.

Next month the sixth grade begins its big unit on American Indians. A temporary reference collection will be set aside for them. Classes will be scheduled to review needed library skills such as use of the card catalog with key subject headings, use of an index, and introduction to special reference tools that will be helpful for this assignment.

FORM 7-9   Sample Monthly Report

your goals. Once again an outline helps. Form 7-10 is an example. Notice that the focus this time is on large events rather than small details. Form 7-11 demonstrates how a report might be written.

```
                    MEDIA CENTER ANNUAL REPORT
                           1981-1982
STATISTICS
  CIRCULATION
    Student
      nonfiction                    8,545
      fiction                      10,609
      periodicals                   1,048
      vertical file                 3,206
    TOTAL                          23,308
    Staff
      nonfiction                    1,217
      fiction                         595
      periodicals                     105
      vertical file                    52
    TOTAL                           1,969
      TOTAL CIRCULATION FOR YEAR          25,347
      LIBRARY SKILLS CLASSES                  46
      TOTAL NUMBER OF BOOKS ADDED            463
      TOTAL NUMBER OF BOOKS DISCARDED         32

STATISTICAL ANALYSIS
Annual circulation figures are lower than last year, reflecting only
the decline in school enrollment. The average of 1½ books borrowed
per student per week is the same as last year. Temporary reference
collections established to meet the needs of large units were not
included in any of these figures. As these special arrangements are
increasing, they will be included in next year's statistics. Teacher
use of professional periodicals is low, although the figure does not
reflect actual use. Faculty members occasionally borrow material
briefly without going through the usual sign-out procedure.
Nonetheless, a program needs to be instituted to stimulate
professional reading.

The library skills classes are those that were scheduled for
instruction, with each lesson averaging 45 minutes. Storytelling
sessions and instruction given during those sessions are not included
in the statistics.

Inventory of the collection is virtually complete. Twenty-one books
are outstanding at this time: 7 are owed by students and teachers, 2
are charged out to a student who has left the state. This leaves 12
books unaccounted for, a remarkably low figure. On the plus side, 5
books that had been reported lost last year were located. The loss
caused by the transfer suggests a need to tighten checks before
students leave the district.
```

```
                           ANNUAL REPORT

ACCOMPLISHMENTS
The weeding of the vertical file was completed in May. The additional
space we obtained means we can now easily add to the collection and
dated material is no longer present.

Teachers have expressed their satisfaction with the way a-v equipment
has been functioning and the speed with which malfunctioning hardware
has been replaced and sent out for repair. The end-of-the-year
cleaning and the summer servicing program are responsible.

Formal library instruction was introduced to second grade. Teachers
and students are enthusiastic.

Volunteers have assumed more paraprofessional jobs, including
filing of catalog cards and maintaining the Sears List of Subject
Headings.

AREAS OF CONCERN
The circulation of software continues to be a problem. Better
controls need to be established. A new form will be designed and the
procedure explained to the faculty at the beginning of the school
year. A written explanation will be distributed at that time.

The lack of volunteers at critical times has affected the efficiency
of the media center. While we are fortunate in the quality and
dedication of all our volunteers, the current economic situation has
meant fewer parents volunteer each year. As a result our coverage is
very thin. When illness or other home problems occur, we lose the
volunteer for several weeks. Projects are then halted and clerical
work backs up. To increase the pool of available volunteers, forms
were given out during kindergarten orientation. A plan to use upper-
grade students as a library council will be attempted.

PROJECTIONS FOR NEXT YEAR
We will evaluate the new software circulation procedure. Teachers
will get a list of all the periodicals we receive in an effort to boost
interest. Meetings will be scheduled with sixth-grade teachers to
determine the best times to have library council. Participating
students would be expected to work 15 minutes before or after school
at least one day a week in addition to time during the school day.

Several volunteers will be assigned to check our collection against
the Elementary School Library Collection. We will then be able to plan
the best way to eliminate any discovered weaknesses.
```

FORM 7-11   Sample Annual Report

BUDGET—A FIVE-YEAR PLAN:

Budget proposals are often tied to long-range planning. You may be asked to prepare a five-year plan for your library media center. Each district will have its own needs and requirements, but here is a basic guide to help you begin.

Divide your plan into categories such as: Personnel, Collection (Print/Nonprint), Equipment, Supplies, and Facilities. A cover sheet should describe and justify the goals you are seeking for each of these categories at the end of the five-year period. Possible goals could be: to meet or exceed A.L.A. standards; to increase the collection in certain areas to meet curriculum needs; to update and modernize equipment for today's computer-oriented society.

Under year one, indicate current conditions. You can use a number of the forms in Section 1 to help you assess your present status. Each succeeding year should show progress toward your ultimate goal. The final column spells out the actual achievement. Be sure that your dollar figures, which will be estimates in any case, reflect probable inflation.

The sample Form 7-12 is a partial selection of items that normally appear on a five-year plan. They become, in effect, a summary statement of your projected budgets. From this plan your Board of Education will be able to see the development you plan for the media center and how much it will cost. The Board can then make its decisions on an informed basis.

At the beginning of each year in the plan, the new budget requests should be accompanied by a statement indicating how well you are progressing. If there are possible savings, such as fewer lost books resulting in a lower dollar figure for replacement or higher costs caused by greater than anticipated inflation, the Board of Education should be informed.

FIVE-YEAR PLAN					
	1 (current)	2	3	4	5	Projected- 5th year
PERSONNEL:	½ - time media spec. ($)	1 full-time med. spec. Total ($)	1 media aide ($) + increment Total ($)	½ media technician ($) + increments Total ($)	½ - time media tech. ($) + increments Total ($)	1 media specialist 1 media aide 1 media technician
COLLECTION: Print Books	8,000 volumes	500 new + 10% replacement Total ($)	500 new + 10% replacement Total ($)	500 new + 10% replacement Total (4)	500 new + 10% replacement Total ($)	10,000 volumes
Newspapers	0	2 — 1 local + 1 national Total ($)	1 — state Total ($)	— Total ($)	— Total ($)	3 titles - National, State and Local
Nonprint Filmstrips	42	250 Total ($)	400 Total ($)	400 Total ($)	400 Total ($)	1,500 filmstrips
Slides	0	250 Total ($)	250 Total ($)	250 Total ($)	250 Total ($)	1,000 slides
Total Collection Cost:		$	$	$	$	
EQUIPMENT: Filmstrip Projector 2x2 slide projector Microcomputer Total Equipment Cost:	0 - media center 6 - classrooms 0 - media center 1 - classrooms 0	1 Total ($) 2 Total ($) 1 Total ($) $	1 Total ($) — $	— 1 Total ($) 1 Total ($) $	— 1 Total ($) 1 Total ($) $	1 — media center 6 — classrooms 2 — media center 4 — classrooms 3 — media center
SUPPLIES: For cataloging, classification, processing & repair of materials - 15% of collection budget	$	$	0	$	$	
FACILITIES: Facilities are adequate for the number of students presently in the school and for the decrease expected within 5 years. Therefore, no change is necessary to the physical structure of the media center.						
TOTALS FOR FIVE-YEAR PLAN:		$	$	$	$	

FORM 7-12   Sample Five-Year Plan

Checklist of Basic Forms

TYPE	On Hand	Can Get	No. of Copies Needed	Doesn't Apply
DISTRICT and SCHOOL FORMS				
Job Description				
Evaluation Form or Criteria				
Selection Policy				
Contract				
Phone Chain				
Absentee Report Method				
MEDIA CENTER ADMINISTRATION FORMS				
Budget Forms				
Purchase Order Forms				
Invoices				
Report Forms				
Repair Requests				
PERSONAL FORMS				
Personal Day Request				
Professional Day Request				
Reimbursement for Professional Day				
Course Approval Request				
Reimbursement for Courses				

FORM 7-1   Checklist of Basic Forms

CLASSROOM REPAIR LIST

Room No. _____   Teacher _____

1. _____
2. _____
3. _____
4. _____
5. _____
6. _____
7. _____
8. _____
9. _____
10. _____
11. _____
12. _____
13. _____
14. _____
15. _____
16. _____
17. _____
18. _____
19. _____
20. _____
21. _____
22. _____
23. _____
24. _____
25. _____
26. _____

       FORM 7-2 Classroom Repair List

LIBRARY MEDIA SPECIALIST'S MONTHLY PLANNING GUIDE

Month _____ **Year** _____

Classes

Clerical Tasks

Special

Library Media Specialist's
Daily Planning Guide

Date: _____

SCHEDULED EVENTS				THINGS TO DO		
Scheduled Time	Event	Prep Time	Priority	Description		Completed

MONTHLY REPORT OUTLINE

MEDIA CENTER REPORT
MONTH, YEAR

I. STATISTICAL INFORMATION
   A. Includes any or all of the following:
      1. Circulation statistics
      2. Number of books cataloged/discarded
      3. Average number of students in media center per day
      4. Number of classes taught
   B. Information may be given on separate attached forms or included in the body of the report
II. ANALYSIS OF STATISTICS
   A. Explain what the numbers mean
   B. Explain special circumstances
      (Not necessary to do this for all statistics)
III. PROJECTS AND POSITIVE OCCURRENCES
   A. Describe new projects briefly
      1. Explain purpose
      2. Estimate time for completion
   B. Report briefly on status of on-going projects
      1. Indicate if on schedule
      2. Give any revised estimate for completion
   C. Report any one-time happenings that reflect positively on the media center program or you
IV. PROBLEMS AND PLANS
   A. Indicate areas of difficulty
      1. Focus on situation
      2. Never mention names or suggest that one person or even a group of people is to blame
   B. Explain how you plan to handle the problem
V. ANTICIPATE NEXT MONTH
   A. Refer back to on-going projects and problem strategy if necessary
   B. Show you can anticipate rather than react to upcoming situations

FORM 7-8   Monthly Report Outline

ANNUAL REPORT OUTLINE

MEDIA CENTER ANNUAL REPORT
School Year

I. CUMULATED STATISTICS

    A. Includes any or all of the following:
        1. Circulation
        2. Average number of students per day
        3. Books/Software added/discarded
        4. Library Skills classes taught
        5. Fines/lost book monies collected
    B. Inventory information
        (Any or all of the above can be attached to the
        report or included in the body)

II. OVERALL STATISTICAL ANALYSIS

    A. Explain meaning of the numbers
    B. Look for strengths and weaknesses

III. ACCOMPLISHMENTS

    A. Major projects completed and their value
    B. Services introduced and an evaluation of
        success/problems
    C   Special teacher/student instruction

IV. AREAS OF CONCERN

    A. Be specific
    B. Give plan to deal with problem

V. PROJECTION FOR NEXT YEAR

    A. Sum up items previously mentioned
    B. General statements about long-range projects

FORM 7-10   Annual Report Outline

Section 8

Forms for Correspondence

I'M AN EXPERT AT HUNT AND PECK.

You must frequently communicate with the world outside your school system to write explanations, complaints, requests, and thank-you notes. As you write, you create an impression not only of your media center, but of your entire school system. You become a force for positive public relations if you do your job well. Samples of how to get the word out succinctly, diplomatically, and effectively are given in this section.

LETTERHEADS (FORMS 8-1, 8-2)

Letters from the media center often go to business offices and should follow correct business form. Handwritten notes are not proper unless they are informal thank-you notes. Your school stationery is what you will most often use. If you would like to give your media center a more distinctive air and you have the money, have letterheads printed by a local print shop. Since they do not design logos, you might use Form 8-1 in combination with your school and library name and address. At current prices, you should be able to get 1,000 printed letterheads and envelopes for just under $100. An alternative for limited budgets is to ask your high school print shop to do the job for you. The charge in this case will be minimal.

For interschool communication, you may want a more informal approach. The Media Center Memo letterhead, Form 8-2, can be used whenever you need to send messages throughout the school. Using a specialized logo regularly, whether it be this form or one of your own design, keeps your message from getting lost in the shuffle. An easily identified symbol will get a quicker response from your faculty.

LETTERS TO PARENTS (FORMS 8-3—8-7)

If you can devise some way to communicate with parents of students entering your school, no matter what the grade, you will have laid the groundwork for pleasant relations. Form 8-3, a sample letter to parents of kindergarteners, shows one way to develop positive attitudes on the part of parents toward the media center and the school.

SOUTHERN BOULEVARD MEDIA CENTER

September 22, 1982

As you know, the kindergarteners come to the media center for story hour every week at which time they learn about books, their authors and illustrators, and hear some old and new stories. This week they will begin signing out books to bring home.

Kindergarten children are allowed to take out one book at a time and keep it for a week. If they are finished with it sooner, they may return it and exchange it for another book. We want to make this a very pleasant experience for them in order to have them begin the lifelong habit of choosing, reading, and enjoying books.

We would appreciate your helping your child find and set aside a special place where library books can be kept, away from younger brothers and sisters and/or pets. If a child gets used to keeping books in one particular place at an early age, the necessity of searching the house for temporarily "misplaced" books throughout the school years can be avoided.

Thank you for your assistance. If you have any questions or comments at any time, I shall be happy to hear from you.

Ruth Toor

Ruth Toor
Library Media Specialist

FORM 8-3   Sample Letter to Kindergarten Parents

Another form of communication that avoids misunderstandings is found in Form 8-4, a letter to parents about Book Fair procedures. This gives a simple explanation of how the Book Fair will be run and what options are available.

Thank-you letters for donations and courtesies are essential. Forms 8-5 and 8-6 show the slight distinctions between a thank-you addressed to a group and to an individual. In your letter be specific as to the gift or favor received and its ultimate purpose.

Sometimes you must communicate unpleasant information. Even so, it must be worded in a way that will encourage cooperation. Form 8-7 shows how you can accomplish this with such a common problem as lost books.

Dear _____,

 Our new Dukane Automatic Sound Filmstrip Viewer
arrived yesterday, and we are just thrilled with it. The
picture on this machine is far superior to our present
viewer and it will be easy for the children to operate. I
know they will get a great deal of pleasure from using this
viewer.

 Please express our thanks to the PTO for this gift.

 Sincerely,

 Ruth Toor

 Ruth Toor
 Library Media Specialist

cc to Superintendent
 Principal

FORM 8-5   Sample Thank-You to PTO

Dear _____,

 Thank you very much for donating the book Ships of the
Twentieth Century to our media center.

 I plan to put it on the browsing table where I am sure it
will be very popular. From there, it will go into our
reference collection.

 I appreciate your thinking of us.

 Sincerely,

 Ruth Toor

 Ruth Toor
 Library Media Specialist

FORM 8-6   Sample Thank-You to Parent

REQUEST FOR REEVALUATION OF MATERIALS (FORM 8-8)

An even more difficult situation arises when a parent objects to materials in your media center. Use your own judgment to determine whether the complaint can be handled on an informal basis. Sometimes a simple explanation can clear the air. If it appears that the parent is determined to pursue the objection, it is necessary to have a written record of the complaint. Most selection policies include such a form. If yours does not, or if you have no selection policy, have the parent complete Form 8-8, a request for reevaluation of materials.

LETTERS TO VENDORS (FORMS 8-9—8-11)

During the course of the school year you will have many occasions to write to vendors and suppliers. One reason is to request material for preview (Form 8-9). Be sure to include the exact catalog number in such a letter. Form 8-10 is a sample of the thank-you that should accompany the return of the materials. This letter is noncommittal. If you have definitely decided for or against purchase, you can be more specific.

Another type of letter, Form 8-11, requests free materials. Any such re-

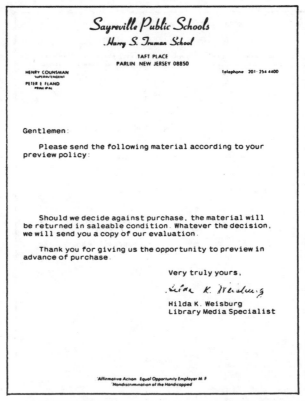

FORM 8-9   Sample Request for Preview

Sayreville Public Schools

Harry S. Truman School

TAFT PLACE
PARLIN, NEW JERSEY 08850

Telephone: (201) 254-4400

HENRY COUNSMAN
SUPERINTENDENT
PETER E. FLAND
PRINCIPAL

Gentlemen:

Thank you for giving us the opportunity to see this material on preview. We will certainly consider it when we prepare our purchase orders.

Very truly yours,

Hilda K. Weisburg

Hilda K. Weisburg
Media Specialist

"Affirmative Action - Equal Opportunity Employer M/F"
"Nondiscrimination of the Handicapped"

FORM 8-10   Sample Thank-You for Preview

SCHOOL DISTRICT of the TOWNSHIP of CHATHAM

SOUTHERN BOULEVARD SCHOOL

192 SOUTHERN BOULEVARD · CHATHAM · NEW JERSEY 07928 · (201) 635-9480

LIBRARY MEDIA CENTER

Gentlemen:

Please send us any free materials you have prepared that would be applicable to teaching about energy in a kindergarten through fifth grade elementary school.

Since there is such an emphasis on teaching students about the energy crisis today, we are trying to build up a file of sources and materials that can be disseminated to the classrooms.

Any help you can give us will be greatly appreciated.

Very truly yours,

Ruth Toor

Ruth Toor
Library Media Specialist

FORM 8-11   Sample Request for Free Materials

quest should be written on school or media center letterhead paper. Many books are available that list sources for free materials. Also be aware of articles and ads in newspapers and professional journals.

LETTERS OF COMPLAINT (FORMS 8-12—8-16)

Letters of complaint should focus on the problem and not turn into an exercise of general mudslinging. Very often you are irate, with good reason, but this should not preclude good manners or obscure your professional judgment. Form 8-12 is a sample complaint letter informing a publisher of a factual error in a book. If you find such an error, you have a professional obligation to inform the publisher. You also need to inform the publisher when product standards have not been met. Publishers cannot correct problems unless they are made aware of their existence. Form 8-13 brings a common problem to a publisher's attention. Generally publishers will replace problem books courteously.

A somewhat more general letter to a publisher is a complaint about current practices. Form 8-14 could also be turned into a letter of commendation had the publisher instituted the practice rather than dropped it. Develop the habit of sending your comments to publishers and other vendors. It's amazing how few letters are required to effect a change.

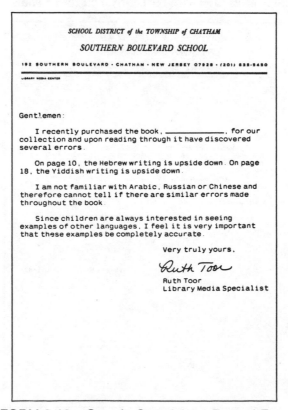

FORM 8-12   Sample Complaint—Factual Error

SCHOOL DISTRICT of the TOWNSHIP of CHATHAM

SOUTHERN BOULEVARD SCHOOL

192 SOUTHERN BOULEVARD · CHATHAM · NEW JERSEY 07928 · (201) 635-9450

LIBRARY MEDIA CENTER

Gentlemen:

    We own a copy of _____
which you published and which I purchased in the "library
edition." This book has circulated only four times and one
section of pages near the front of the book has torn loose
from the binding.

    I'm very unhappy about this, because with the rising
cost of books today and the decreased amount of money I
have available to spend, I can't afford to purchase books
that begin to fall apart after such a few circulations.

    Is there anything you can do about this problem? I look
forward to hearing from you.

                                Very truly yours,

                                Ruth Toor

                                Ruth Toor
                                Library Media Specialist

FORM 8-13   Sample Complaint—Defective Material

SCHOOL DISTRICT of the TOWNSHIP of CHATHAM

SOUTHERN BOULEVARD SCHOOL

192 SOUTHERN BOULEVARD · CHATHAM · NEW JERSEY 07928 · (201) 635-9450

LIBRARY MEDIA CENTER

Dear _____,

    I am very disappointed to see that you have stopped
using the Cataloging-in-Publication data on the back of
the title page on many of your new children's trade books.

    I have found it to be very helpful and a big time-saver
when I order books and do original cataloging. Is there a
reason you no longer use the CIP data? I would be
interested in hearing from you about this.

                                Sincerely,

                                Ruth Toor

                                Ruth Toor
                                Library Media Specialist

FORM 8-14   Sample Complaint—Current Practices

Problems often develop with a-v hardware and software. Form 8-15 requests a replacement for damaged malfunctioning software. In this case, both a check and the damaged loop accompany the letter. When requesting a software replacement, check company policy through the catalog or a sales representative to determine what must be done. Sometimes, for any number of reasons, a-v hardware that was purchased proves to be unacceptable. In such a case you must ask the vendor for an adjustment as in Form 8-16. Do not think that because you ordered the materials you have no recourse. It never hurts to ask.

SCHOOL DISTRICT of the TOWNSHIP of CHATHAM

SOUTHERN BOULEVARD SCHOOL

192 SOUTHERN BOULEVARD · CHATHAM · NEW JERSEY 07928 · (201) 635-9480

LIBRARY MEDIA CENTER

Gentlemen:

   We are returning the 8 mm film loop "The San Francisco Earthquake" from the set Film Highlights of Modern History – The Early 1900's which is damaged and does not work in the projector, together with a check for $10.00.

   Please send us a replacement loop.

   Thank you.

                                        Very truly yours,

                                        Ruth Toor

                                        Ruth Toor
                                        Library Media Specialist

FORM 8-15   Sample Complaint—Replacement Request

SPECIAL LETTERS (FORMS 8-17, 8-18)

As a library media specialist, you might find yourself writing to various authors and illustrators on behalf of your students. Form 8-17 is a letter to an author informing him of the selection of one of his books as a school favorite. A special request is made in the last paragraph. Letters to authors are generally very favorably received, although there are always exceptions.

Form 8-18 thanks a colleague for a pleasant visit. It is a courtesy that should not be overlooked.

SCHOOL DISTRICT of the TOWNSHIP of CHATHAM

SOUTHERN BOULEVARD SCHOOL

192 SOUTHERN BOULEVARD · CHATHAM · NEW JERSEY 07928 · (201) 635-5450

LIBRARY MEDIA CENTER

Gentlemen:

Last September, we received a shipment of Audiotronics
HS-15 headphones to go with junction box listening
centers. They were used during most of the school year.

This September these headphones were found to be
inoperable and we sent them out to be repaired. They were
recently returned to us unrepaired because it would cost
more to fix them than it would to replace them.

Our district a-v coordinator says that the headphones
were not suitable for student use and were poorly
constructed.

These headphones were purchased on the advice of your
representative who knew what use would be made of them.

I feel that an adjustment or replacement should be made
on this order and look forward to your prompt reply.

Very truly yours,

Ruth Toor

Ruth Toor
Library Media
Specialist

FORM 8-16   Sample Complaint—Request for Adjustment

SCHOOL DISTRICT of the TOWNSHIP of CHATHAM

SOUTHERN BOULEVARD SCHOOL

192 SOUTHERN BOULEVARD · CHATHAM · NEW JERSEY 07928 · (201) 635-5450

LIBRARY MEDIA CENTER

Dear _____,

I thought you would be interested to know that in a
contest held at our elementary school in which students
vote for their favorite book,
_____ was the winner in our upper
team consisting of fourth and fifth graders.

The children have all gone on to and enjoyed reading the
other books in this series.

This is our seventh annual contest, and our upper team
students design Southern Boulevard Book Award Medals to
place on the award-winning book jackets.

Would you be willing to autograph our copies of
_____ if we send them to you?

Sincerely,

Ruth Toor

Ruth Toor
Library Media
Specialist

FORM 8-17   Sample Letter to Author

SCHOOL DISTRICT of the TOWNSHIP of CHATHAM

SOUTHERN BOULEVARD SCHOOL

192 SOUTHERN BOULEVARD · CHATHAM · NEW JERSEY 07928 · (201) 635-5450

LIBRARY MEDIA CENTER

Dear Mrs. James,

I just wanted to let you know how much I enjoyed
visiting your media center last week. It is such a warm and
friendly place that I can easily see why the children love
it.

I was impressed with all of your efforts to sell your
program to your teachers. From what I was able to see, it
looks as though you've been extremely successful at it.

The media center handbook you compiled seems to be a
very good way of explaining your programs and services. I
saw a number of ideas I'm looking forward to trying.

Thanks again for all your time and trouble. It was fun
meeting you and seeing your school.

                                Sincerely,

                                Ruth Toor

                                Ruth Toor
                                Library Media
                                Specialist

FORM 8-18   Sample Thank-You to a Colleague

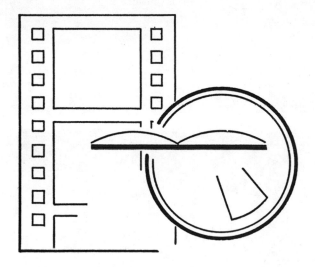

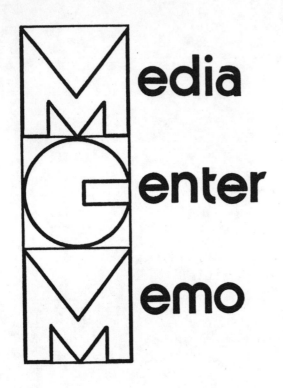

FORM 8-2   Media Center Memo Heading

Dear Parents:

Next week we are having a Book Fair at our Media Center. Classes are scheduled for two visits. The first visit gives children a chance to make a list of titles they would like to purchase. They make their purchases during the second visit.

Please take the time to discuss with your child the list he or she brings home. Cross off any titles you do not want your child to buy and be sure the list is brought back to school along with the money. Checks can be made out to

_____.

If you would like to see the books, you are welcome to visit the Media Center during the following times:

You are also welcome to make purchases yourself while you are here.

The Book Fair provides children with an opportunity to build and extend home libraries. Reading is a habit and having a home library encourages the development of that habit. Books also make excellent, and inexpensive, gifts.

If you have any further questions, please don't hesitate to call me.

Sincerely,

Library Media Specialist

Dear _____,

    I am sorry to inform you that your child, _____
owes the following material to the IMC (library):

    On three occasions reminders were sent from the IMC to
the class. In addition, teachers repeatedly remind
students whose names appear on overdue lists to return the
material.

    Please help your child search for the above items. If
they are not located, it will be necessary to bill you.

              Sincerely,

              Library Media Specialist

              FORM 8-7   Lost Book Notification

CITIZEN'S REQUEST FOR RECONSIDERATION OF INSTRUCTIONAL MATERIALS

Author, Editor or Compiler _____   Type of material _____

Title _____

Publisher _____

Request initiated by _____

Telephone _____   Address _____

Complainant represents

_____ Himself

_____ (Name of organization) _____

1. To what material do you object? (Please be specific; cite pages, filmstrip frames, etc.) _____

_____

2. What do you feel might be the result of a student becoming involved with this material in a learning situation?

_____

3. For what age group would you recommend this material? _____

4. Is there anything good about this material? _____

_____

5. Did you read the entire book? (or examine all of the audio-visual material)? _____

_____ If not, what sections? _____

6. Are you aware of the judgment of this material by literary critics? _____

_____

7. What do you believe is the theme of this material? _____

_____

8. What would you like the school to do about this material? _____

_____ Do not assign it to my child

_____ Withdraw it from all students as well as my child

_____ Send it back to the proper department for reevaluation

9. In place of this book (or audio-visual material) would you recommend other material which you consider to be of

superior quality? _____

_____

_____   _____
Date   Signature of Complainant

FORM 8-8   Request for Reevaluation of Materials

Section 9

Forms for End-of-Year Activities

IMPOSSIBLE!
I STILL HAVE 6 MORE WEEKS
OF WORK TO DO.

Closing the media center for summer vacation requires tight organization, close scheduling, and extra help. The more efficient you are in June, the smoother your September reopening will be. Organize your staff in order to gain control over books, materials, and equipment as they are returned for end-of-year processing. Forms are given for scheduling, recalling, and inventorying materials and equipment as well as for a culminating activity, either a thank-you party or a trip, which provides your helpers with the incentive for future service.

STAFFING FOR INVENTORY (FORMS 9-1—9-3)

Try to get extra volunteers to help you during this very busy time. Form 9-1, Request for Helpers, is one way to draw in people who have not previously volunteered. Once these forms have been returned, correlate them with your regular volunteer schedule and prepare an inventory helpers schedule, Form 9-2. Post the schedule prominently so you can make last-minute additions and also see who will be coming each day. Your regular helpers may notice gaps in the time schedule and volunteer for extra duty. Form 9-3 should be sent out a week before the inventory to remind people of when they are scheduled.

MEDIA INVENTORY (FORMS 9-4—9-9)

Before you begin the inventory of your book collection, it is a good practice to check the current operational status of all a-v hardware. If you have the time and staff, this job may be done earlier in the year. Whatever your

```
┌─────────────────────────────────────────────────────────┐
│                   SOUTHERN BOULEVARD SCHOOL               │
│   SBS              IT'S INVENTORY TIME                    │
│                                                          │
│                 Can you help us do the job?              │
│                                                          │
│   The Library Media Center will be taking inventory from June 8th to │
│   June 12th. Many parents are needed to assist our regular helpers │
│   in this important task.                                │
│            Will you volunteer a few hours of your time?  │
│                  NO EXPERIENCE NECESSARY                 │
│                                                          │
│   If each of you can give one morning or afternoon, the job can be │
│   accomplished. (Of course, if you can give more time than that, │
│   we'd be even more delighted.)                          │
│                                                          │
│   Please fill out the form below                         │
│   and return it to the school.                           │
│                                                          │
│   Thank you                                              │
│                                                          │
│   Ruth Toor                                              │
│   Ruth Toor                                              │
│   Library Media Specialist                               │
│                                                          │
│   . . . . . . . . . . . . . . . .                        │
│                                                          │
│   Yes, I want to help with the inventory.                │
│                                                          │
│                             A. M.          P. M.         │
│                          _____    _____      │
│       Monday, June 8     _____    _____      │
│       Tuesday, June 9    _____    _____      │
│       Wednesday, June 10 _____    _____      │
│       Thursday, June 11  _____    _____      │
│       Friday, June 12    _____    _____      │
│                                                          │
│   Name_____        Telephone_____        │
└─────────────────────────────────────────────────────────┘
```

FORM 9-1   Sample Request for Helpers

circumstances, it must be done at least *once* during the year. The faculty must be informed which type of equipment should be returned when. Form 9-4 gives that information. Be prepared to make personal reminders also.

Form 9-4 calls teachers' attention to a new sign-out procedure for the end of the year. This procedure requires a separate sign-out sheet for each type of equipment. Form 9-5 allows teachers to check out already inventoried hardware on an as-needed basis and keep it until the last day of school if necessary. When equipment is returned, it is a simple matter to check it back in quickly and store it for the summer.

```
┌─────────────────────────────────────────────────────────┐
│              SOUTHERN BOULEVARD MEDIA CENTER             │
│                              May 29, 1981                │
│                                                          │
│   Thank you for offering to help us take inventory. We will be │
│   looking forward to seeing you on ____Wednesday____, June _10_ │
│   from _9:00_ to _11:30 AM_.                             │
│                                                          │
│                                                          │
│                              Ruth Toor                   │
│                              Ruth Toor                   │
│                              Library Media Specialist    │
└─────────────────────────────────────────────────────────┘
```

FORM 9-3   Sample Thank-you for Volunteering/Inventory Reminder

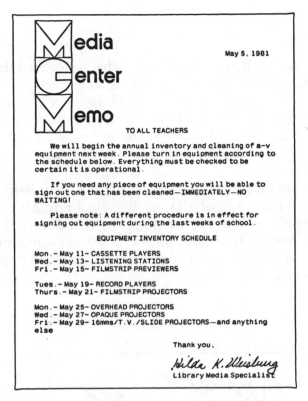

FORM 9-4   Sample Media Inventory Schedule

As equipment is turned in, it will need to be checked in an orderly sequence. Form 9-6 shows the operational checks performed on cassette recorders and Form 9-7 shows similar checks on filmstrip projectors. The simple check method enables you to stop the operation and pick it up again at any time. The forms allow you to both clean the equipment and check its performance. Design additional forms according to your specific equipment needs.

As you take inventory, note the record of repairs on the Individual Equipment Repair Record cards (Form 4-9) kept during the year. Then summarize malfunctions found during the end-of-the-year hardware inventory on Form 9-8. Attach this to your annual report (Form 7-10). You won't be adding to the text of the report, but you will be documenting the scope of your responsibilities.

A software inventory is conducted in the same way as your book inventory, by checking the shelf list cards against the media stored on the shelves. In addition, you must insure that none of the components of a set is missing. Give Form 9-9 to your volunteers and let them fill in the blanks as they take this inventory. If they cannot locate the producer and catalog number on the box, you can get that information later yourself. Use the list to reorder missing materials immediately so they will be on hand for your September opening.

END-OF-THE-YEAR NOTICES (FORMS 9-10—9-14)

Alert faculty and students to the end-of-the-year schedule. Form 9-10 is a sample memo stressing the altered conditions under which students may use the media center as well as giving circulation cut-off information.

In addition to the regular overdue notices, you must now inform teachers of student obligations. Form 9-11 serves this purpose. For teacher obligations, you can use Form 3-30 or 3-31 or Form 9-12 which is specifically tailored to your end-of-year operations.

Allow a few days for students to locate or pay for missing material. Then send parents Form 9-13 as a final attempt to collect anything still outstanding. If a receipt is needed when a student pays for lost material, use Form 3-34. For your own records, or if it is required, enter the amount on Form 3-33. Form 9-14 clears students of media center obligations and permits them to receive their report cards.

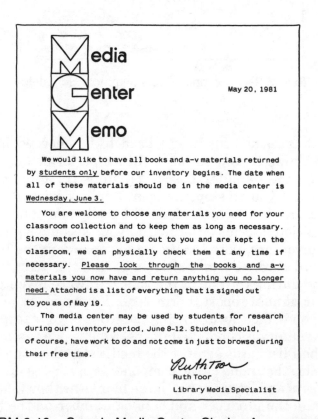

FORM 9-10   Sample Media Center Closing Announcement

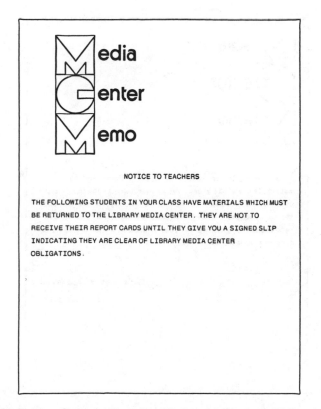

FORM 9-11   Sample Teacher Notice of Student Obligations

INVENTORY REPORT (FORM 9-15)

After the book inventory has been completed, you can record the results on Form 9-15 as you make a final check of the shelves. No matter how much clerical help you have, you still need to verify that the books marked "missing" on the cards really are missing. This form takes into account "found" books, those listed as missing previously that are now back on the shelves. Lost book totals usually neglect this statistic. In order to record these figures, provide volunteers with tally sheets to mark "found" books while taking the inventory.

FORMS FOR THANKING YOUR SUPPORT STAFF (FORMS 9-16—9-21)

After the inventory take the time to thank students and parents for all of the help they have given. A tea or party serves as an expression of your appreciation for their efforts. Plan ahead but schedule the festivities for a date when your inventory has been completed. Form 9-16 is a sample invitation.

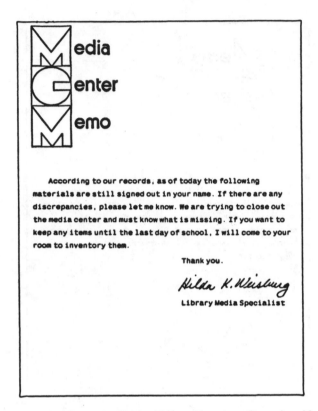

FORM 9-12   Sample End-of-Year Teacher Overdue Notice

Another type of thank-you is a special trip. Student volunteers will need permission from parents. Many districts have their own forms, but a reproducible permission slip is provided in Form 9-17 if you need it.

Whatever your culminating activity, a certificate can be presented as a more formal thank-you. While certificates may be purchased from library supply houses, you can just as easily make your own. Form 9-18 is a reproducible award for adult volunteers and can be personalized with the name of your school. If you can't do the calligraphy to write the school name on the top line, perhaps a skilled faculty member will help. Your finished certificate will look more professional by doing so. Form 9-19 is a simple certificate for student volunteers and allows you to write the number of years the student has served.

Instead of certificates, you may wish to give students a special award. Supply houses carry a variety of pins suitable for Library Council members. However, if your school has a button-making machine, you can give awards that are not only original, inexpensive, and attractive, but also extremely practical.

Form 9-20 shows a selection of 11 designs for special awards. Adapt any of these using your school initials. After they have been presented, students can wear their buttons whenever they are on duty in the media center. They

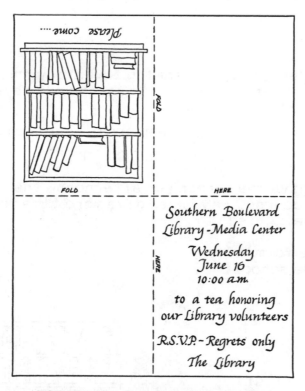

FORM 9-16   Sample Invitation to Tea

will be easily identifiable as experienced helpers. You might even use different color backgrounds to indicate the number of years of service.

To keep your volunteers coming back, an effective public relations device is a personal thank-you letter. Form 9-21 can be sent to all volunteers or just to those who have made a special effort during the inventory period.

TEACHER EVALUATION OF LIBRARY MEDIA CENTER PROGRAM (FORM 9-22)

The end of the year is a natural time to assess the success and/or failure of your complete program. The only way to get this evaluation is to impose on your teachers who are also busy with final activities and ask them to take a few minutes to complete Form 9-22. You need this feedback to see if your perceptions are in line with the way the faculty sees you and to identify areas that may need strengthening. You might have better results if you distribute the form at your last faculty meeting of the year.

IT'S INVENTORY TIME

Can you help us to do the job?

The Library Media Center will be taking inventory from _____
_____. Many parents are needed to assist our regular helpers
in this important task.

Will you volunteer a few hours of your time?

NO EXPERIENCE NECESSARY

If each of you can give one morning or afternoon, the job can be
accomplished. (Of course, if you can give more time than that,
we'd be even more delighted.)

Please fill out the form below
and return it to the school.

Thank you,

Library Media Specialist

*   *   *   *   *   *   *   *   *   *   *   *   *

Yes, I want to help with the inventory.

	A.M.	P.M.
Monday, _____	_____	_____
Tuesday, _____	_____	_____
Wednesday, _____	_____	_____
Thursday, _____	_____	_____
Friday, _____	_____	_____

Name _____   Telephone _____

FORM 9-1   Request for Helpers

LIBRARY INVENTORY HELPERS SCHEDULE

	Monday	Tuesday	Wednesday	Thursday	Friday
A.M.					
P.M.					

FORM 9-2   Library Inventory Helpers Schedule

_____
(date)

Thank you for offering to help us take inventory. We
will be looking forward to seeing you on

_____, _____ from

_____ to _____

_____

Library Media Specialist

FORM 9-3   Thank-You for Volunteering/Inventory Reminder

Year _____

Year-End Hardware Sign-Out Sheet
Type _____

Code Number	Teacher Name	Date Out	Date In

Year _____

Operational Check and Maintenance
Cassette Recorders

Code Number	Checked In	Head Cleaned/ Demagnetized	FF and Rewind	Volume	Play	Record	Earphones	Status

FORM 9-6   Operational Check and Maintenance Form—Cassette Recorders

Year _____

Operational Check and Maintenance
Filmstrip Projectors

Code Number	Checked In	Lenses Cleaned	Lamp Checked	Fan Checked	Interior Cleaned	Status

FORM 9-7   Operational Check and Maintenance Form—Filmstrip Projectors

EQUIPMENT REPAIR SUMMARY

TYPE OF EQUIPMENT/CODE	REASON FOR REPAIR

FORM 9-8   Equipment Repair Summary

Date _____

SOFTWARE INVENTORY

TYPE	CALL #	MISSING/DAMAGED COMPONENTS	PRODUCER	CATALOG #

FORM 9-9   Software Inventory

Dear _____ ,

    I am sorry to inform you that your child, _____ ,

has not returned the following to the media center:

      Title   Date Due   Cost

    Please send the material or the cost listed above by

_____ , or it will be necessary to withhold your

child's report card.

                            Very truly yours,

                            Library Media Specialist

FORM 9-13   Parent Notice of Lost Books

_____ has been cleared
of all Media Center obligations and may receive
his/her report card.

_____

FORM 9-14   Media Center Obligation Clearance

Year _____

Media Center Inventory Summary

CLASSIFICATION	Lost and Paid	Unaccounted For	Other	Total Lost	Found
Fiction					
TOTAL FICTION					
000's					
100's					
200's					
300's					
400's					
500's					
600's					
700's					
800's					
900's					
Biography					
TOTAL REGULAR NONFICTION					
Reference					
Special Collections					
TOTAL NONFICTION					
GRAND TOTAL					

FORM 9-15   Media Center Inventory Summary

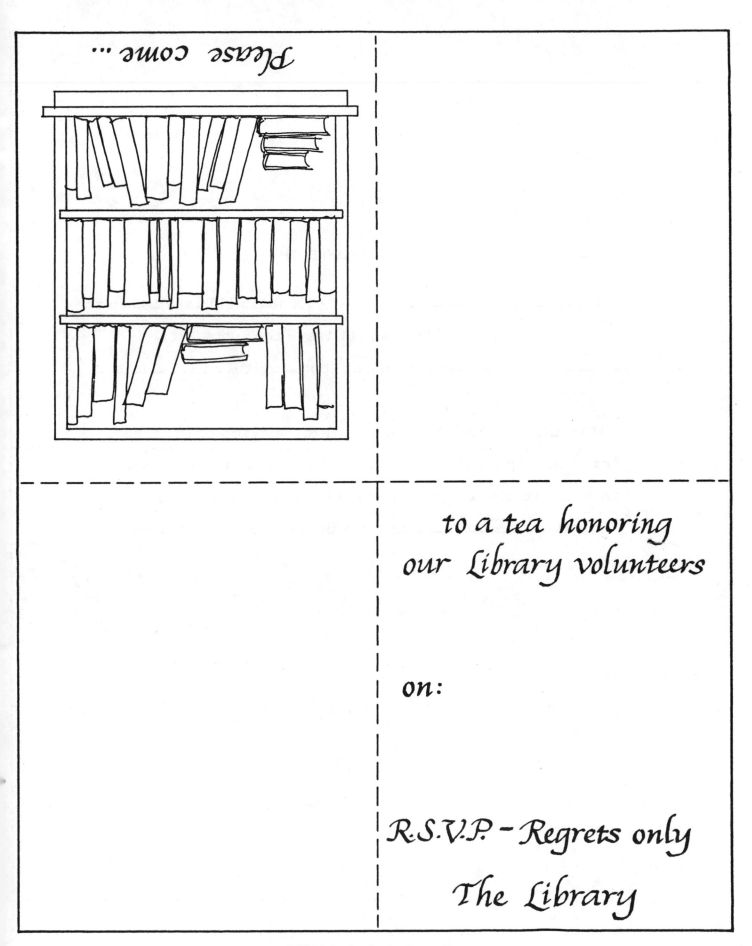

Please come ...

to a tea honoring
our Library volunteers

on:

R.S.V.P. - Regrets only

The Library

FORM 9-16   Invitation to Tea

PERMISSION SLIP

On _____ the Library Council will take a trip to

_____ . The bus will leave the school at

_____ and return at approximately _____

This trip is intended as a reward for service to the school

this year. The cost of the trip is _____ which is due with

this signed permission slip no later than _____ .

My child _____ has permission to go on this

trip.

(Signature) _____

FORM 9-17   Permission Slip

Media Center

Volunteer Service Award

Thank you for your help!

_____
Date

_____
Signature

A
Certificate of Service

is presented to

_____

for _____ year of volunteer work in

_____

_____
Principal

_____
Library Media Specialist

FORM 9-19   Student Certificate of Service

230

FORM 9-20   Special Award Buttons

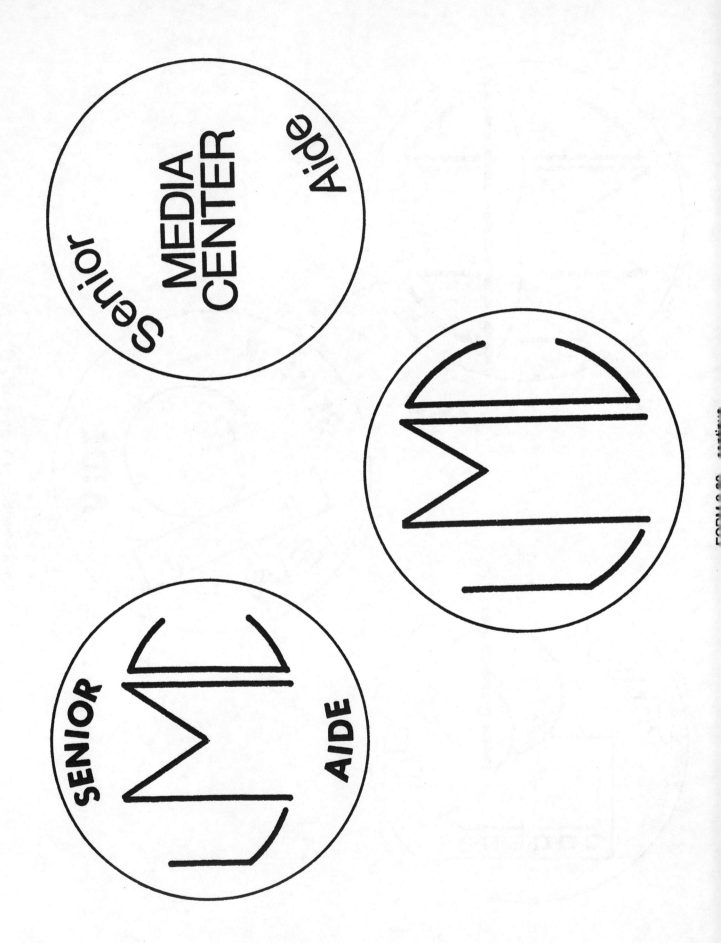

232

SENIOR

MEDIA CENTER AIDE

SENIOR

AIDE

SENIOR

AIDE

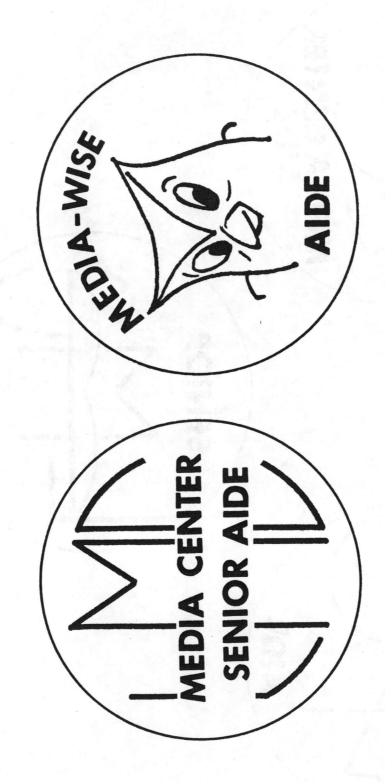

FORM 9-20   continued

Dear _____.

   Thank you for all your time and effort during the end-of-year inventory. It is a huge job that would be impossible to do properly without the support and cooperation of volunteers like you.

   I know what a busy schedule you have, and I truly appreciate your willingness to devote time to the Media Center. You have been a tremendous help.

   I hope you have a pleasant summer, and I look forward to seeing you again in the fall. Once more, I thank you.

                                   Sincerely,

                                   Library Media Specialist

        FORM 9-21   Thank-You to Volunteer

Teacher Evaluation of Library Media Program

	Always	Some-times	Rarely	Never
1. The library media center offers me access to a variety of materials with which I can supplement my instructional program.				
2. My requests for materials have received prompt attention.				
3. I have received prompt and courteous help from the library staff.				
4. I have had help in the creation of materials for my program.				
5. My suggestions for improving the media program have been welcomed.				
6. I have been offered opportunities to preview new materials.				
7. I have been asked for suggestions about the purchase of new materials.				
8. I have been instructed in the use and operation of audio-visual equipment.				
9. Audio-visual equipment has been available when I needed it.				
10. Problems with audio-visual equipment have been attended to promptly.				
11. Reserve collections have been set aside at my request.				
12. Bibliographies have been prepared at my request.				
13. Transparencies and other specialized teaching aids have been prepared at my request.				
14. I am regularly informed of additions to our collection.				
15. I find the professional collection useful.				
16. My students need more instruction in library skills.				
17. My students need more general help from the library than they now receive.				
18. The media center provides both the space and the equipment that allows for small-group work.				
19. The media center is an attractive, relaxing place that is conducive to study.				

20. Please use the space below for any comments or suggestions to expand upon or add to the questionnaire.

Section 10

Forms for Professional Growth and Development

I WONDER HOW MUCH I'VE GROWN?

Aside from your responsibilities for organizing and operating a successful media center, you must also take the time to evaluate, maintain, and extend your development as a professional. You must stay current with the changes in librarianship and be able to promote your own abilities forthrightly. Forms in this chapter include resume and job application, personal records of courses taken and conventions attended, as well as demonstrations of professional expertise.

JOB SEEKING FORMS (FORMS 10-1—10-3)

Your resume should be kept up to date. Preparing one is a form of self-evaluation. If you are unsure about how to begin, consider a resume workshop given by a local college or university or read one of the many books on the subject. However you might find some simple guidelines sufficient.

A resume will not necessarily get you a job, although it may cost you one, so don't spend an inordinate amount of time in preparation. Keep it brief; one page is best. Keep it neat; note the format in Form 10-1 as to margins, use of capital letters, and spacing. Make it sell; use active verbs to list accomplishments. Make it specific; avoid describing daily activities but highlight the unique.

There are many ways to locate job openings: state hotlines, newspaper and professional journal classified advertising, and inside information from your colleagues. Form 10-2 is a sample letter of application done in a full-block format, a distinctive style of business letter. The first paragraph briefly states the job you are seeking and where and when you heard about it. The second paragraph is a short hard-sell without qualifying words such as "think," "hope," or "feel." The final paragraph emphasizes your interest in the position and ends on a positive note.

```
                              Resume

                    JANE DOE
                              Street Address
                              City, State, Zip Code
                              (Area Code) Phone Number
        OBJECTIVE:
                    To organize a media center program that
                    supports and enriches the entire school
                    curriculum.

        EXPERIENCE:
          19 __-      School Name, Town, State
          date        Developed library skills curriculum for
                      grades K-6. Trained staff of volunteers.
                      Instituted storytelling program for
                      grades K-4. Expanded a-v program. Trained
                      faculty in video-taping operations.
                      Participated in liaison with other
                      district media specialists.

          19 __-      School Name, Town, State
          19 __       Worked with volunteers. Taught library
                      skills. Developed Occupational
                      Literature File.

        EDUCATION:
                      M.L.S. University Name, State, year of
                      graduation.

                      B.A. University Name, State, year of
                      graduation.

        CERTIFICATION:
                      State Certification in Media

        PROFESSIONAL
        ACTIVITIES:
                      State Media Association

                      Workshops and/or Inservice Programs
                      Presented
                        Date     Subject

        REFERENCES:
                      References will be furnished on request.
```

FORM 10-1   Sample Resume

Writing a follow-up letter after an interview is often overlooked and yet it may be the deciding factor in your getting the job. The sample in Form 10-3 reminds the interviewer of the highlights discussed and reaffirms your interest in the position.

FORMS FOR PROFESSIONAL DEVELOPMENT (FORMS 10-4—10-7)

Additional courses help you to keep up with changes in librarianship. Whether you take them at many different colleges or universities or are matriculated in one program, keep an ongoing course record using Form 10-4. This will aid you in preparing your resume, remembering where to obtain transcripts, and advising your district of current graduate credits for salary adjustment purposes.

Taking courses is expensive. Besides the tuition, you have fees, books, transportation, and incidentals such as meals and photocopying. Even when

Name
Address
Home Telephone
Business Telephone

Date

Superintendent of Schools
Address

Dear _____ :

In reply to your advertisement in the (newspaper) of Sunday, (month), 19 __, for a library media specialist, I am enclosing a copy of my resume.

My experience as a (grade level) library media specialist gives me the background to meet the needs of your students and faculty. I look forward to proving to you the accuracy of this assessment.

I can arrange my schedule to be available for an interview at your convenience and look forward to hearing from you.

Very truly yours,

FORM 10-2 Sample Letter of Application

Name
Address
Home Telephone
Business Telephone

Date

Superintendent of Schools
Address

Dear Dr. Jones:

I enjoyed speaking with you on June __, 19 __ when you interviewed me for the position of elementary school media specialist.

Your awareness of the importance of school media centers makes this opening highly desirable. I was particularly pleased to discover that we share similar views concerning the integration of library skills with regular classroom assignments.

Thank you for such a pleasant and informative interview. As a result of our conversation, I am even more interested in the position and look forward to hearing from you in the near future.

Sincerely,

Home telephone number:

FORM 10-3 Sample Thank-You for Interview

you are reimbursed (and many people are not), the entire cost is never covered. Form 10-5 allows you to document your costs for your records and those of your school district as well as for the Internal Revenue Service.

Another way to keep abreast of happenings in the library field is to attend conventions, conferences, workshops, and institutes. These also have hidden costs. Form 10-6 gives you a statement of expenditures for your files.

At some time you may be asked to present a workshop or give an in-service program. Use Form 10-7 to document these professional activities. It is helpful when updating your resume and very effective when left at the end of a job interview.

* * * *

Forms can overwhelm or simplify. The idea is to choose those that suit your situation and your problems. They are the foundation of all of today's required documentation. It takes time to become adept at recordkeeping, but with practice you can be an efficient manager and show yourself to the best advantage.

RECORD OF COURSES

University/College	Course Number	Title	Credits	Grade

FORM 10-4   Record of Courses

Course Expense Record

Semester _____ Year _____

COURSES: (Titles) 1. _____	
2. _____	
3. _____	
SCHOOL–ADDRESS _____	

TUITION	$
FEES	$
	$
BOOKS (Title and cost)	
	$
	$
	$
	$
	$
	$
	$
COURSE INCIDENTALS	$
	$
TRANSPORTATION	
Round trip miles × Cost per mile × Number of trips	$
Tolls, round trip × Number of trips	$
Parking fees	$
TOTAL	$
AMOUNT REIMBURSED	– $
NET COST	$

FORM 10-5   Course Expense Record

Convention Expenditure Record

Sponsoring Group _____   Date(s) _____

Location

Basic Costs			Optional Extras		
Registration	$		Banquet(s)	$	
Hotel	$		Luncheon(s)	$	
Transportation	$		Special Tours	$	
Air/Car	$			$	
Tolls	$			$	
Total	$		Total	$	

Professional Purchases					
For media center (List item and cost)			For personal use (List item and cost)		
	$			$	
	$			$	
	$			$	
Total	$		Total	$	

Extra Convention Costs			Cost Summary		
Tax Deductible			Total Basic Costs	$	
Meals	$		Total Optional Extras	$	
In-City Transportation	$		Professional Purchases	$	
Tips	$		For media center	$	
Total	$		For personal use	$	
Non–Deductible			Extra Costs		
Entertainment	$		Tax Deductible	$	
Film	$		Non-Deductible	$	
Souvenirs	$		Grand Total	$	
Total	$		– Amount Reimbursed	$	
			Total Costs	$	

FORM 10-6   Convention Expenditure Record

RECORD OF WORKSHOPS

DATE	SPONSOR	PERSON IN CHARGE	TITLE/SUBJECT	TIME	NUMBER PRESENT	COMMENTS/EVALUATION

FORM 10-7   Record of Workshops

Appendix

Directory of Names and Addresses of
Commercial Suppliers of Library Forms

General Library Supply Houses:
      Brodart, Inc.
      1609 Memorial Ave.
      Williamsport, Pennsylvania 17707 (800) 233-8467

      Demco, Inc.
      Box 7488, 2120 Fordem Avenue
      Madison, Wisconsin 53707 (800) 356-8394
              or
      Box 7767, 5683 Fountain Way
      Fresno, California 93727

      Gaylord Bros. Inc.
      Box 4901
      Syracuse, New York 13221 (800) 448-6160

      Highsmith Co. Inc.
      P.O. Box 25
      Fort Atkinson, Wisconsin 53538 (414) 563-9571

Awards: some of the general library suppliers plus:
      Beckley-Cardy Co.
      There are 9 regional offices serving different areas of the country.
      Call toll-free (800) 543-6660 to find your regional office.

      Fordham Equipment & Publishing Co.
      3308 Edson Avenue
      Bronx, New York 10469 (212) 279-7300

Clip Art:

      Creative Art Productions, Inc.
      22552 King Richard Court
      Birmingham, Michigan 48010

      Library Educational Institute, Inc.
      R.D. 1, Box 219
      New Albany, PA 18833 (717) 746-1842

Displays—Create Your Own:
    Dick Blick
    P.O. Box 1267
    Galesburg, Illinois 61401 (800) 447-8192

Displays—Holiday
    Beckley-Cardy Co. (details under *Awards*)

    Dennison Manufacturing Co.
    300 Howard Street
    Framingham, Massachusetts 01701 (617) 879-0511

Library Promotional Material:
    American Library Association
    Public Information Office
    50 E. Huron Street
    Chicago, Illinois 60611 (312) 944-6780

    Children's Book Council, Inc.
    67 Irving Place
    New York, New York 10003 (212) 254-2666

    Robert Jacobson: Design
    1504 W. University Heights Drive North
    Flagstaff, Arizona 86001 (602) 774-1137

    Upstart
    Box 889
    Hagerstown, Maryland 21740

Posters:
    American Library Association (details under *Library Promotional Material*)

    Caedmon
    1995 Broadway
    New York, New York 10023 (800) 223-0420

    Demco, Inc. (details under *General Library Supply Houses*)

    Giant Photos
    Box 406
    Rockford, Illinois 61105

    Robert Jacobson: Design (details under *Library Promotional Material*)

For materials to meet special needs, see the Annual Buying Guide included in *School Library Journal* (Ex.: April, 1981).

INDEX